COMPUTER-BASED SYSTEMS

John Race was born in 1934 and educated at Bromsgrove School and Merton College, Oxford, where he was a Classical Postmaster. After serving in the Royal Air Force he worked in the practical implementation of computer systems with Courtaulds, IBM, BOAC, IPC, British Oxygen and Rank Xerox. In 1975 he was awarded a Ph.D. by Brunel University for work on pattern recognition and artificial intelligence and he now teaches there while continuing research, writing and consultancy.

He is married (to another Oxford Classics graduate) and has three children. He holds a private pilot's licence and is particularly interested in the use of computers in aviation.

TEACH YOURSELF BOOKS

COMPUTER-BASED SYSTEMS

John Race

TEACH YOURSELF BOOKS
Hodder and Stoughton

Fifth impression 1982

*Copyright © John Race
1977*

ISBN 0 340 20772 8

*Printed in Great Britain
for Hodder and Stoughton Educational,
a division of Hodder and Stoughton Ltd,
Mill Road, Dunton Green, Sevenoaks, Kent
by Richard Clay (The Chaucer Press) Ltd, Bungay, Suffolk*

Contents

Acknowledgements

I should like to thank IBM, ICL, and Honeywell Ltd. for information on their products and services, and for permission to reproduce pictures.

The programs given in examples were run on the Brunel Computer Unit's ICL 1900 and PDP11, and on the UCC's IBM/360 model 65.

The material has been drawn largely from personal experience at those companies for whom I have worked as employee or consultant, including Courtaulds, IBM, BOAC (now British Airways), BOC, Rank Xerox, and RACAL. In addition, I have used news items from *Computing* (incorporating *Dataweek*), *The Computer Journal*, *Datamation*, *Computer Weekly*, and many others. This book also owes a debt to the EUP *Data Processing* by K. N. Dodd.

The index was produced using one of the many facilities of Dr. C. Reynolds' CODIL language.

1

The Purpose of this Book

This book was written with three kinds of people in mind.

Firstly, there are those who do not actually work with computers themselves, but would like to know more about these machines which pay them, tax them, send them bills, find them friends of the opposite sex, put them on aeroplanes, and even catch them out in crime. Just as pedestrians are well advised to have a good working appreciation of the ability of the motor car to accelerate, brake and turn, so people on the receiving end of the other important machine of our era—the computer—would be well advised to know its powers and limitations. For example, a friend of mine in America had the harrowing experience of receiving hospital bills for surgery on his wife, month after month, when the bill had been paid and his wife died: the hospital simply told him to ignore them, since this was due to an error in the system. The most effective way of dealing with this situation was to submit a change of address to the computer so that the bills were sent to some non-existent place.

Another kind of reader may wonder what the life of a computer professional is like. Who are these mysterious *programmers* who appear to lead such exciting lives, and earn large salaries? Is a *systems analyst* a kind of super-programmer, or a psychiatrist for computers, or what? These readers may wonder whether they themselves might make a career in this field. It is hoped that this book may help them to decide, by describing the work of the various kinds of computer professional, their exhilarations and frustrations, and the skills which they need to do their jobs. There is no doubt that the 'computer man' is rather a specialist and although in the early days of computers it was expected that young men and women would move through computing to other parts in their organisation, it now seems that the great majority of those who enter the field remain in it. So be warned! If as a result of reading this book you decide to work with computers (and many of us feel this is the only real occupation for a rational human being) you are likely to have made a decision for life.

The third kind of reader is the student at school, technical college or university who expects to obtain a professional qualification for which a knowledge of computers is required. This book should help to give them a context for the more formal computer science they are learning, in the sense that the emphasis here is on applications of computers to real life. Some samples of examination questions are included in Appendices 3–5 and these may be of general interest in that they show the range of knowledge expected of a computer professional. (For these readers the next chapter may contain material which is already familiar, but they may nevertheless find interesting the 'top-down' descriptive approach which has been used.)

Though we may study computer-based systems for personal reasons like those given above, inevitably we find ourselves faced with some wider issues. The computer is a machine which embodies the whole Western attitude to life: the belief that we can make mathematical or symbolic models not only of physical nature, but also of our relationships with each other, and between organisations: that these models can be rigorously defined, and that such models, realised as computer systems, can replace the original relationships in part or in whole. Instead of my arguing with the village grocer for a side of ham 'on tick', I use a credit card. The decision to allow credit is mechanised, using sound statistical principles, and the book-keeping and arithmetic is done for us both, so we have more time to do other things. Our relationship is different: argument and embarrassment—and human contact—are reduced.

This book is not the place to embark on philosophy or sociology, but as we look at the various systems we should perhaps ask ourselves what the implications are. It seems strange to us now, but when town gas was first introduced widely in Victorian times, the word 'gas' was associated with everything that was modern: Dickens' 'all is gas and gaiters' had the connotation 'up to the minute'. Similarly 'computer' was, in the 1960s, synonymous with excitement and controversy. Computer jokes appeared in magazines and an ugly style of lettering, supposedly associated with computers, was used on shop fronts. Fortunately, like the 'glamour' of gas, the glamour of computers too has now rubbed off, and they are less in the public eye. Yet in fact their numbers and power are greater by far now than in the days of popular attention. The variety of ways in which they are used has been extended. This parallels the growth in military and civil applications of nuclear energy: there is much less popular excitement today over anti-missile missiles, multiple independently-targeted re-entry vehicles, atomic-powered human heart pacemakers and the widespread use of atomic fuel, than over their small beginnings in the 1950s.

In the early days of computers they were described as 'giant brains', and there was much speculation on whether they could think. Nowadays it is more usual to dismiss them as 'giant morons', that 'can only do exactly what they are told'. This is just as muddle-headed. Admittedly the computer derives its abilities from instructions ('program') written by a human being, but such a program may in fact tell the computer to modify its responses to circumstances which the programmer did not *specifically* foresee: hence there is no paradox in a computer playing better chess than its programmer. Similarly if a computer decides I am not a credit-worthy person and withdraws my credit card, it may do so by applying rules which it had evolved for itself (based for example on my age, my pattern of paying, my indebtedness, etc.) after being programmed to *evolve* such rules. The problem is that I do not know who to argue with: if the grocer had refused me the ham, at any rate I could have asked him on what basis he made the decision and perhaps queried his facts, or called him names. There is no point in doing this to the computer or its programmer. And yet from the point of view of the community the computer credit system may be far more effective than the old method of individual haggling: protecting traders and honest customers, and cutting down on book-keeping. Computer systems illustrate better than almost anything else the dilemma in which we find ourselves: is efficiency attainable without the alienation of the individual? And if not, what is the right compromise point?

There are other situations in which the computer is indeed limited to the role of a giant moron, but is powerful because it has access to quantities of facts, and can correlate them: in a simple-minded way, no doubt, but with such speed as to make possible massive investigations which armies of clerks with thousands of filing cabinets could never tackle. It is said that the Austro-Hungarian Empire was 'despotism tempered by inefficiency': similarly many people have been saved from social or legal disapproval simply because their bank statements, marriage certificates, National Insurance cards, hotel registrations, tax declarations, hire purchase forms, and road fund applications have never been compared. If every citizen had a single record containing all such information, on a central computer, blameless individuals would perhaps find form-filling quicker and easier and cheaper, but when the computer, however moronic, attempted to reconcile some of the entries brought together for the first time, the *less* blameless among us might regret it, and our legal system would be swamped with cases of bigamy, tax evasion, and illegal immigration. Once again, there are sensible and compelling reasons for the building of these 'data-bases', and it is the duty of both computer professional and layman to be aware of the issues involved and to ensure that whenever a computer-based system is introduced, it fits within an acceptable framework of human responsibilities and objectives. We may have to surrender some of the 'freedom of inefficiency', but it must be deliberate. This is discussed more fully in Chapter 7, 'Wider Issues'.

Something should be said about what this book is *not* intended to be. In the first place it is not a primer on electronic design for computers. In the First World War, pilots were discouraged from knowing much about their engines because it would make them nervous to realise how complicated and liable to breakdown they were. But this is not the reason why this book does not take the covers off the computer: modern computers are exceptionally reliable. It is just that a detailed knowledge of their electronic working is not essential for an understanding of this book, interesting though the subject is in its own right. What the reader is asked to take on trust is that letters, figures, and other symbols can be encoded into an electrical or magnetic representation, and that in this form they can be manipulated by electronic circuitry: added, multiplied, stored, and finally translated back again in a form human beings can use. Now that pocket calculators are in common use, few people will find this difficult to accept.

The study of the electronics involved is of course fascinating in its own right, and if the reader wants to know just *how* symbols are translated and manipulated electronically, he or she will find *Electronic Computers*, in this series, of interest. But as a first lesson in 'systems thinking', we must be able to regard machines as 'black boxes' which we understand very well *functionally*, but whose detailed workings are the province of another specialist.

To give a simple example, if we were presented with a box with a light and three switches:

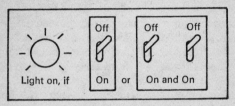

Fig. 1 *Black box*

we need not demand to see the circuit diagram (shown below) to appreciate how the box is supposed to behave.

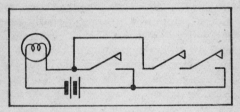

Fig. 2 *Circuit diagram*

Secondly, this book is not a treatise on computer programming. To understand computer-based systems does indeed require some knowledge of the role of the programmer and this will be covered in the next chapter. For a fuller treatment of programming the reader is referred to *Computer Programming/Fortran* and *Computer Programming/Cobol* (Teach Yourself Books).

2

Systems, Systems Analysts, Programmers, Operations Staff, and the Computer

Systems

We really should begin with the definition of the word 'system' itself. Unfortunately this is used by computer people in more than one way:

(a) To describe the actual computer equipment or 'hardware', as in the phrase, 'this *system* must be installed in a room with air conditioning'. The main IBM computer range is known as *System/370*.

(b) In the phrase 'operating system', the word describes a special general-purpose program usually provided by the manufacturer of the computer, which occupies only part of the computer's capacity and is responsible for making it easier to use. Programmers who specialise in this kind of program are known as 'systems programmers', and are expert at developing or modifying operating systems so that the 'application programs'— the ones that actually print payslips or do other specific jobs—can run as efficiently as possible, by making use of the operating system's services such as checking that a file of product information is the correct one to use this week.

But in this book we are concerned with a 'system' in

the sense of the whole combination of computer, programs, forms, human procedures, communications and so on needed to carry out a particular job. Here is a possible definition:

> 'A *system* is an organisation of people, each with defined responsibilities, and using appropriate methods, to achieve together a defined set of objectives.'

Note: families and democracies are not 'systems' in this sense because their members' objectives and responsibilities are not formally defined. But the definition probably includes totalitarian states, and armies in wartime.

Of course a *computer-based system* is one in which the computer occupies a central place in the methods used, and the inclusion of the computer among the repertoire of available methods has brought about a change in the power and scope of systems comparable with that introduced into warfare by gunpowder or into industry by steam.

One should also note that the systems we are mainly concerned with when we talk about 'computer-based' systems, are to do with information handling. This places very little restriction on their scope since in the modern Western world many more people handle information for their living (turning knobs, reading, writing, etc.) than handle physical objects. But however much their power and scope have increased, systems should be described first in terms of their objectives and of the responsibilities of the *people* involved. We may say loosely that 'the computer has the responsibility for checking the credit-worthiness of any customer before his order is accepted', but in reality the computer must be acting as an extension—almost like an artificial arm—of some human being's responsibility, perhaps in this case the credit control manager. It follows that the rules by which the computer carries out credit checking must be understood and agreed with, if not actually specified by, the credit control manager: and that in so far as the computer makes errors (works to the wrong rules), the credit control manager should accept responsibility for putting them right and preventing future recurrences.

Unfortunately there are systems in which the computer carries out functions which are *not* on behalf of some identifiable individual who accepts responsibility for them, and it is in these cases that difficulties arise: where we are likely to hear a clerk say 'It's that stupid computer again!'

Conversely there are computer systems in which the human beings feel a sense of partnership with the machine: they do their distinctive tasks, which the computer cannot, such as asking after a customer's wife and family, while the computer supports them with *its* contribution: providing information, doing calculations quickly and accurately, printing order forms and so on. Their ideal relationship might almost be that of a ploughman and his horse.

The systems analyst: exploiter of opportunities to make use of computers in systems

Whether a computer-based system turns out to be a success or a failure depends very much on the *systems analyst*. This man or woman is usually a member of a small team called in by the management of the organisation, to study a particular area with a view to introducing the use of computers. Originally the idea was that the analysts would 'analyse' the present system, by recording document flows, information stored, and so on, and then translate all this into a computer equivalent. This process was given the ugly name of 'computerisation'. For certain kinds of task such as the calculation of wages and salaries, or preparing actuarial tables, this approach is just about defensible. But many opportunities were missed for applying the real power of the computer because the old system, now 'computerised', had been limited, by the means available, to achieving only a part of the objectives. A sales accounting department, for example, might be theoretically responsible for obtaining customer payment as quickly and fully as possible, but in practice it was preoccupied just with preparing invoices against deadlines: if the analyst simply analysed what was done, he would end up with a computer-based invoicing system which might or might not be more cost-effective than the old one; but if the analyst looked at the true objectives, the result might be that the computer produced a new style of invoices, for the first time designed and timed to stimulate customer payment as well as being accurate. Moreover, the clerks in the department might now be busier than ever—but doing a different job, perhaps telephoning customers to hasten payment, and resolving queries quickly and amicably. The results would be much better in terms of benefits to the company and job satisfaction within the department. Even if the objectives of the new system are just the same as the old one, it is likely that bringing in a computer will require human jobs to be redefined. Norbert Wiener described this target—the proper allocation of work between people and computer so as to achieve partnership rather than antagonism—as 'the human use of human beings'.

The systems analyst not only investigates the opportunity for computers to increase the achievement of objectives in some area, and devises a new system in which people may take new responsibilities and will use the computer as a major tool in carrying them out, but is also responsible for bringing this new system into being. It may be that the organisation already has a computer with capacity to spare for this new job: if not, he will have to look into the possibility of installing one, or using a bureau, and of including these costs in his calculations of benefits. From experience, experiment, reading, and calculations he or she will set up on paper a description of the proposed new system in operation—giving estimates of the type and size of the machine required, the work-load on the people involved, the layout of the new computer-produced forms ('output'), and the forms needed by the computer for information presented to it ('input'). The computer processing has to be defined and estimates made of how best this has to be carried out, i.e. what programs will have to be written.

After this paper working model has been proved practical and its costs reasonable in comparison with the benefits expected from better achievement of objectives, and when the amount of effort to install the system has been taken into account, a senior manager or group of managers will decide whether to go ahead: there may be many other projects, such as building a new plant, on which time and money could be spent instead, even if this one is profitable when considered in isolation.

The programmer is waiting to get started

Even after this decision the analyst's task is only just beginning. But there now appears on the scene the *programmer*, who will be responsible for actually getting the computer to carry out the processing specified by the analyst. In the next section of this chapter we see how the grand design of the analyst is picked up by the programmer, and the parts of it that describe what the computer's contribution is to be, are translated into a set of computer processing rules—a program.

The reader may have noticed that instead of starting with electronics and working through computer logic and programming to systems and their place in an organisation, we have gone the other way—'top-down', rather than 'bottom-up'. This approach has the drawback that the reader will constantly be asking questions such as: 'You talk about a computer holding information, but just exactly how is this done?' There are two reasons for structuring the explanations in this way. Firstly, it is perhaps easier to read a book with questions in one's mind—providing they get answered in the end!—than with information in one's mind whose relevance is not yet apparent. The other reason is that the systems analyst and programmer tackle—or should tackle—their tasks in a similar 'top-down' way, and if you follow the logic of this book's structure you may get a feel for the systems approach.

So let us consider what the systems analyst is likely to ask the programmer to do, at the top level. We might well take a sales accounting department again as an example. Let us suppose there is a small firm making crockery, which it sells direct to hotels and restaurants. After a consignment of tea-pots or cups has reached a customer the accounts department sends him a bill, or 'invoice', and eventually expects to receive a cheque or postal order back. The firm has a computer and a team of one analyst and one programmer. (A big company may have twenty analysts and thirty programmers, or more. Women do well in both roles, and in this book 'he' should be taken as 'he or she' where appropriate.) The analyst has decided that the computer will be required to *accept* (as 'input') forms of five types:

- information about goods offered for sale, and changes to information
  e.g. Large Teapots at 50p: Breakfast Cups now 20p.
- information about customers and changes
  e.g. Mr. Gibson, the Lobster Pot Café, Mevagissey.
- notifications of delivery
  e.g. One Large Teapot and six Breakfast Cups, to the Lobster Pot.
- notifications of cash received
  e.g. £1·70 from Lobster Pot Café.
- adjustments
  e.g. £0·20 credit to Lobster Pot Café (previous breakage).

He also has specified that the computer is to *produce* two forms (as 'output'):

● Invoices

 e.g. 'To Lobster Pot Café, please pay £0·50 in respect of
 teapot delivered on . . . £1·20 for cups . . .

● Statements

 e.g. showing all deliveries, invoices and payments, on the
 Lobster Pot and all other accounts, for the last month.

We can regard the computer part of the system as a 'black
box' which we can draw as in Fig. 3. This chart is a
simplified 'systems flow chart' using conventional symbols
for documents, processing, and manual operations. It does
not tell us anything about the information content of the
various forms, or in what way the information coming out
of the computer box is to be based on the information going
in.

 The analyst must make this clear before the programmer
can start work. He may proceed as follows:

Specifying the computer part of the overall system

On the last Friday of the month the system is to prepare the
invoices, giving the most up-to-date customer and product
information (e.g. if a form had been raised a few days earlier
to say that the Lobster Pot was now owned by Mrs. Thomas,
this information must replace whatever was previously held,
e.g. owner was Mr. Gibson), or if large teapots are to cost
55p, the price change must be reflected in invoices produced
thereafter.

 The invoices must show the customer name and address,
all the deliveries made to the customer during the month,
the calculation of quantity × price worked out: VAT added,
totals calculated, and all these details printed on the invoices.

 Lastly we want statements to be prepared on the same day
giving the complete state of play on all customers—recording invoices sent, payments made, adjustments, changes and
so on.

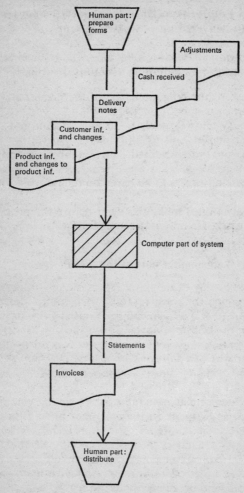

Fig. 3 *The computer part of a system as a 'black box'*

One way of tackling this would be to use the human beings to assemble the forms in the right order for the computer to use, with copies of product information as required (since no doubt several different customers will have received Large Teapots during the month). Note that it becomes necessary to re-sequence customer information ahead of product information.

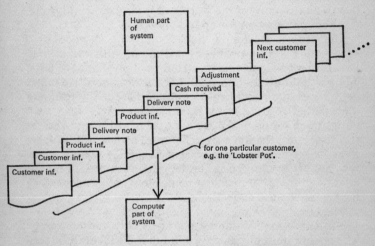

Fig. 4 *Assembling forms ready to prepare invoices and statements— a clumsy approach*

This will involve a mammoth clerical copying, sorting, and filing operation at the end of the month. It would be much better if the computer could hold *static* information, such as the fact that Mrs. Thomas is now the owner of the Lobster Pot and will probably remain owner for a year or two, so that this fact would not have to be presented to the computer system afresh each month.

Similarly, although we do not want to hold delivery note

and other *transient* information permanently, it would be very much more convenient if such forms could be presented in any order to the computer during the month, and be checked for mistakes, such as containing references to customers the computer system has no record for. If there was an error, we would then have (usually) plenty of time to correct it and present it again before the end-of-the-month run. So, again, we would like the computer system to make provision for the storing of information: this time, *transient* information for up to a month.

The analyst must now think how the computer is to achieve this. Very probably he will end up with the idea of having two *files*, one holding all information about *products*, and one holding all information about *customers*. He might decide to make room in the customer file for the transient information relating to each customer as well: then such information would be deleted after the monthly run whereas the static information (Mrs. Thomas, owner: the Lobster Pot . . .) would remain unchanged until a change came through. (It would also be just as valid an approach for the analyst to decide to define a completely independent third file called 'Transient Transactions' or some such.)

The files must be organised so that the right customer and product information can be got at quickly and efficiently. The analyst must also bear in mind that the forms produced by *people* will need to be in a medium, or converted to a medium, which the *computer* can read.

For the present we shall ignore the physical nature of the computer's reading devices and files. But we can now expand the earlier flow chart to show the computer part of the system in more detail (see Fig. 5).

I hope it is becoming clearer how the 'top-down' approach to systems design operates. We continually postpone decisions on points of detail as long as possible by defining 'black boxes' which carry out broad functions we see need to be done (like storing information, or converting infor-

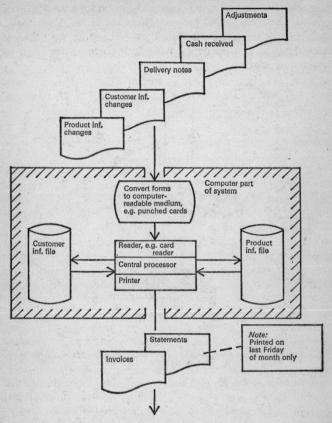

Fig. 5 *The 'black box' opened up*

mation on 'human' forms into a computer-readable medium).

The contents of the box called 'computer part of the system' may actually be physically found in the computer department itself, although some of the devices do not much resemble the symbols used, and it might be that the logically separate customer and product files could be, physically, contained in a single unit. Equally the computer could have other devices, not needed for Sales Invoicing, but used in some other task.

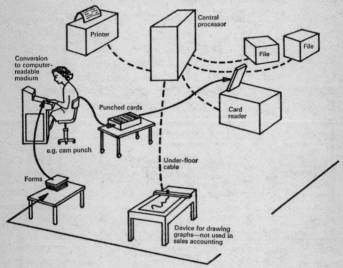

Fig. 6 *The* **physical** *units in the computer installation*

It should be noted that in most computer installations like the one above, one will see a number of apparently independent metal units. They are in fact connected by cables under a false floor, and all of them together make up the computer. These cables are, so to speak, the channels along which pass the information symbolised by arrows in the preceding systems flow charts—except that information on the form, after conversion to a computer-readable medium (paper tape, punched cards, tape cassette) travels to the reader in a box or on a trolley.

Let us say that the computer-readable medium in our example is to be punched *cards*. These will be described in more detail later.

The central processor

Like a spider in the centre of its web, the central processor (CPU) controls all the peripheral boxes by sending Input/Output (I/O) signals through the cables which effectively say things like 'read another card and send me back the information on it', or 'print a line of characters as follows: "TO MRS. THOMAS, THE LOBSTER POT, MEVA-GISSEY" . . .'. It is also capable of holding information from the reader or files in its own local storage or (a useful American imported term) *memory*, and working on it.

A global, but incomplete specification is written for the computer processing

The analyst now concentrates his attention on what sequence of signals to reader, printer and files, and what operations on memory the central processor should go through to carry out its part in the sales accounting system. Again, looking at the problem from a 'top-level' viewpoint and ignoring all the details such as whether dates should appear as DD.MM.YY or MMM,DD,YYYY, and how VAT should be computed, he could express its required overall behaviour as a diagram (see Fig. 7).

Please check that this block diagram expresses the function of the 'black box' in Fig. 5.

Note: This symbolism is different from the 'systems flow chart' shown earlier, and is known as a 'logic block diagram', in which the lines do not represent the flow of documents or other information media, but the sequence in which operations are carried out. As a matter of fact this diagram is

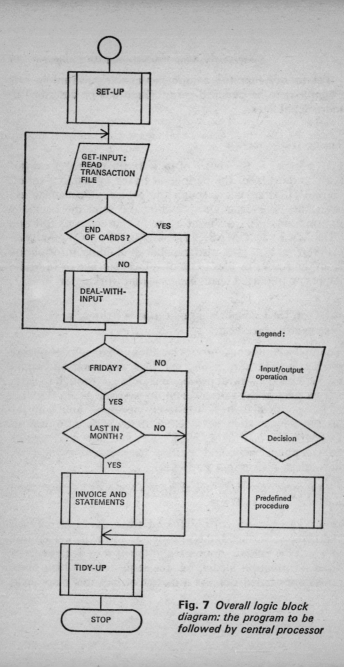

Fig. 7 Overall logic block diagram: the program to be followed by central processor

sometimes given other names, such as 'program flow chart', and so on: it does not matter very much what we call these charts so long as we do not confuse it with the *systems* flow chart. Do not mix, like different trading stamps, a decision diamond (Fig. 8(a)) (which belongs in a *logic block diagram*)

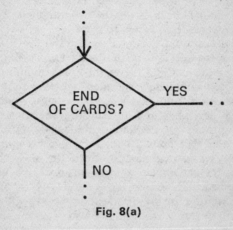

Fig. 8(a)

and a file storage symbol (Fig. 8(b)) (which belongs in a *systems flow chart*)

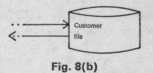

Fig. 8(b)

on the same page!

The sales accounting logic block diagram prepared by the analyst is a collection of black boxes, each implying an enormous amount of detailed processing work. Until this work has been specified by the analyst, obviously the new computer-based system is incomplete. He must take each of

the boxes in turn and enlarge it into a logic block diagram
in its own right, and so on until he is laying out, for example,
details of how the calculation of VAT is to be done. He must
also specify the contents of the customer and product files,
and the layout of the five forms coming in and the two
coming out, as punched cards and printer lines respectively.
After all this has been done, the programmers will have a
full specification from which to work.

At one time it was considered undesirable for the computer
programmer to start until *all* the detailed processing had been
specified by the analyst. 'Never start programming until the
job has been completely specified' was the motto, and a
healthy reaction from days when the analyst would make a
few design decisions, and let the programmer set to work
translating these into computer programs, only to have to
tell him later that he had had to change his mind, with a
consequent waste of time and effort. But this motto does
mean that the activities of the systems analyst cannot easily
be overlapped, and there is a danger that the programmer will
be sitting waiting for the specification, and then the systems
analyst will be waiting for him to finish programming it.

An incomplete program *can* be written to incomplete specifications

This problem has been overcome to a large extent by the
'top-down' approach *applied within programming itself*. It is
in fact possible to write a program which corresponds to the
program block diagram above. It would look something
like the example in Fig. 9.

*Please go through this program and check for yourself that it
is equivalent to Fig. 7.*

Two questions come to mind. Since a computer has to be
told precisely what to do, how can it make any kind of sense
out of 'PERFORM SET-UP', when the procedure SET-UP

```
PROCEDURE DIVISION.
START-RUN.
    PERFORM SET-UP.
GET-INPUT.
    READ TRANS-FILE AT END PERFORM TEST-FOR-LAST-
    FRIDAY.
    PERFORM DEAL-WITH-INPUT.
    GO TO GET-INPUT.
TEST-FOR-LAST-FRIDAY.
    COMPUTE DAY-ONE-WEEK-AHEAD = TODAYS-DAY-
    NUMBER + 7.
    IF FRIDAY THEN IF DAY-ONE-WEEK-AHEAD IS
    GREATER THAN LAST-DAY-OF-THIS-MONTH THEN
    PERFORM INVOICE-AND-STATEMENTS.
    PERFORM TIDY-UP.
    STOP RUN.
```

Fig. 9 *Program corresponding to logic block diagram in Fig. 7.
COBOL*

is still undefined? Secondly, what is the point of producing
this incomplete program?

We can answer these questions as follows. The programmer can put in his program 'dummy' procedures
SET-UP, DEAL-WITH-INPUT, INVOICE-AND-STATE-
MENTS, and TIDY-UP which do not do any more than
print out that the computer began the procedure concerned,
and of course if the full set of actions to be done had been
there, would have carried them out. It is rather like testing
a car for its resistance to collapse in a crash, with dummy
passengers in the seats. Now the computer has a complete
program in which every situation is covered—after a
fashion.

Secondly, in answer to the question, 'why bother anyway?', although the program written at this stage has no
chance of actually billing MRS. THOMAS for the Large
Teapot she received, the programmer has the opportunity
to test the main structure of the proposed program, and to
ensure that he has overcome the many small administrative

problems that arise in the early stages of developing programs—many of them tied up with using the *operating
system* mentioned earlier. (It is helpful, but it is sometimes
rather pernickety about the way it is used!) Once the programmer has got this very simple program working, he will
substitute the real procedures for the dummies, progressively,
as the analyst is able to pass him the specifications for the
processing. He can also copy the skeleton program as many
times as there are dummies, and develop and test the real
procedures each in their own 'skeleton', independently and
in parallel. The programmer does not just need specifications
for the processing to be done on information, i.e. the *procedures*, but he also wants to know the *lay-outs* of the
information itself, coming in from the reader, and the files:
and of the information to be printed on the printer. Once
again, if some of this is not yet available, the programmer
can set up some dummy lay-outs temporarily, in order to
satisfy the computer's demand to be told exactly how its
information is to be organised: and give it the truth later.
This information is formalised in the DATA DIVISION in
the example which follows.

Below is shown the computer program SALE01 written
as a first attempt at the Sales Accounting processing. We
know it is only an outline, but we also know how subse-
quently to transform the outline into actuality, black box
by black box, as the analyst completes his work.

It may be of interest that this simple example program
took five attempts to get working, over a period of a week.

Attempt 1: The Input/Output Section was accidentally
omitted. The wrong sort of quotation marks (' instead of ")
were used.
Attempt 2: The program appeared to be grammatically correct but the operating system would not accept it because
the name was too long.
Attempt 3: The program was accepted but would not work

because the procedure SET-UP failed to OPEN FILES, since the instruction, following a NOTE, was also taken as a note. A colleague also pointed out the need for an AD-VANCING in the print instruction to prevent all information being printed on the same line.

Attempt 4: The program was found ungrammatical in that in COBOL ADVANCING 1 LINE should be ADVANC-ING 1 LINE*S*. To be grammatical in both English and Cobol I changed it to 2 LINES.

Attempt 5: Successful.

```
IDENTIFICATION DIVISION.
PROGRAM-ID.
    "SALE01".
AUTHOR.
    J P A RACE.
REMARKS.
    THIS PROGRAM GIVES THE BARE BONES OF THE
    PROCESSING TO BE DONE BY THE COMPUTER. WHEN
    THE ANALYST HAS SPECIFIED THE SYSTEM IN FULL
    DETAIL I SHALL BE ABLE TO REPLACE THE PROCEDURES
    WHICH ARE JUST DUMMIES AT THIS STAGE BY THE
    PROPER ONES. IN THE MEANTIME THIS PROGRAM
    SERVES TO TEST THE MAIN PROCESSING LOGIC.
ENVIRONMENT DIVISION.
CONFIGURATION SECTION.
SOURCE-COMPUTER. ICL-1903.
OBJECT-COMPUTER. ICL-1903. MEMORY 16000 WORDS.
INPUT-OUTPUT SECTION.
FILE-CONTROL.
    SELECT TRANS-FILE ASSIGN TO CARD-READER 1.
    SELECT PRINT-FILE ASSIGN TO PRINTER 1.
DATA DIVISION.
FILE SECTION.
FD PRINT-FILE.
01 PRINT-RECORD.
    02 COMMENTARY              PIC X(120).
FD TRANS-FILE.
01 FORM-RECORD.
    02 FORM-INF               PIC X(80).
WORKING-STORAGE SECTION.
77 TODAYS-DAY-NUMBER          PIC 99.
```

```
77 LAST-DAY-OF-THIS-MONTH        PIC 99.
77 DAY-OF-THE-WEEK-TODAY         PIC 9.
   88 FRIDAY              VALUE 6.
77 DAY-ONE-WEEK-AHEAD            PIC 99.
```

```
PROCEDURE DIVISION.
START-RUN.
    PERFORM SET-UP.
GET-INPUT.
    READ TRANS-FILE AT END PERFORM TEST-FOR-LAST-
    FRIDAY.
    PERFORM DEAL-WITH-INPUT.
    GO TO GET-INPUT.
TEST-FOR-LAST-FRIDAY.
    COMPUTE DAY-ONE-WEEK-AHEAD = TODAYS-DAY-
    NUMBER + 7.
    IF FRIDAY THEN IF DAY-ONE-WEEK-AHEAD IS
    GREATER THAN LAST-DAY-OF-THIS-MONTH THEN
    PERFORM INVOICE-AND-STATEMENTS.
    PERFORM TIDY-UP.
    STOP RUN.
```

```
SET-UP.
    OPEN INPUT TRANS-FILE.
    OPEN OUTPUT PRINT-FILE.
    MOVE "SET-UP PROCEDURE ENTERED" TO PRINT-
    RECORD.
    WRITE PRINT-RECORD AFTER ADVANCING 2 LINES.
    MOVE 27 TO TODAYS-DAY-NUMBER.
    MOVE 31 TO LAST-DAY-OF-THIS-MONTH.
    MOVE 6 TO DAY-OF-THE-WEEK-TODAY.
DEAL-WITH-INPUT.
    MOVE "DEAL-WITH-INPUT PROCEDURE ENTERED" TO
    PRINT-RECORD.
    WRITE PRINT-RECORD AFTER ADVANCING 2 LINES.
INVOICE-AND-STATEMENTS.
    MOVE "INV-AND-STATMT PROCEDURE ENTERED" TO
    PRINT-RECORD.
    WRITE PRINT-RECORD AFTER ADVANCING 2 LINES.
TIDY-UP.
    MOVE "TIDY-UP PROCEDURE ENTERED" TO PRINT-
    RECORD.
    WRITE PRINT-RECORD AFTER ADVANCING 2 LINES.
    CLOSE TRANS-FILE.
    CLOSE PRINT-FILE.
```

Fig. 10 *The program with dummy procedures and layouts added to make it workable*

Writing and testing the program

But it is now time to use the above example to gain insight into the programmer's activities.

We can visualise him sitting at a desk with the block diagram (Fig. 7) in front of him, and a pad of specially printed paper on which to write the program. An example is given in Appendix 1. He will use a soft pencil and have an eraser to hand—it is easy to make mistakes. Close by he will have some manuals which remind him of the rules for program writing for the particular kind of computer he is dealing with: a sort of grammar which tells him what phrases and words he can use and what he cannot. The example given above was written according to the grammatical rules of COBOL, but there are several others, just as there are different human languages. Other computer languages include BASIC, FORTRAN, PL/1, and ALGOL.

When he has finished he has a number of forms in front of him, which have to follow much the same path as the forms we envisaged in the sales accounting system: they must be converted into a medium which can be handled by the computer reader, say punched cards. Then the central processor must call for the information on the cards, and when it has assembled the whole lot, must actually treat the information as a series of instructions which it must now carry out. If, as usually happens the first time we present the central processor with a program, there are errors in it, it will notify us of the errors and only try to carry out the program if the errors are fairly trivial. Errors will very likely be notified by the central processor sending messages to be printed out on the printer. The programmer will get back all these messages, and will make whatever corrections are necessary, and try again.

Perhaps the processor finds nothing wrong, but when it tries to carry out the program, unexpected things happen: the printer produces complete gibberish instead of (as in the

example) 'TIDY-UP ENTERED' at the expected place.
Once again the programmer has to find out what is wrong
and put it right, and in a complicated program this is sometimes far from easy. The 'top-down' approach helps here
too, in that he can usually pin-point the *procedure* in which
the trouble is occurring. If he develops different procedures
independently, he will also be able to continue testing the
others while investigating an obscure fault in one.

When finally the program works, and the analyst and the
programmer together have incorporated every detail of the
Sales Accounting system in the program, and tested it with
all possible cases on some imaginary customers (not the real
Mrs. Thomas, in case some lurking fault sent her a bill for
a million Large Teapots), the program will be ready to use
in hot blood. Effectively, the programmer's forms will (in
their computer-readable medium, e.g. cards) precede the
Customer Information, Product Information, and other
Sales Accounting cards whenever the Sales Accounting
system is to be run on the computer. The processor will
recognise the first batch of cards as instructions for itself,
and when they are all stored in its own memory, will start
executing them. It will carry out the procedure SET-UP,
and then start calling for the other, Sales Accounting, card
information from the reader, which are in effect *transactions*.

As each FORM-RECORD comes in, the program will
direct the central processor to carry out the procedure
DEAL-WITH-INPUT, which in fact at this stage only
causes the processor to send the line 'DEAL-WITH-INPUT
PROCEDURE ENTERED' to be printed on the printer,
and then return (GO TO GET-INPUT) to read some more.
When the reader has no more sales information left (AT
END PERFORM TEST-FOR-LAST-FRIDAY) the pro-
cessor switches to a different procedure which tests to see if
it is the right occasion to produce invoices and statements.
To do this it has to compare today's day number with 6, the

value of Friday, and then check that, if today is Friday, it is also the *last* Friday in the month.

Obviously at the beginning of the computer run, during SET-UP, the real day number, date, and days in the month should have been obtained. One way would have been to have designed a document on which this information could be written, and have it read as the very first input card. Alternatively, we could use the helpful Operating System— the small program which sits in a corner of the processor and is responsible for providing such general services—to make these values available. (The operating system itself would of course need to get them from somewhere at the start of the day, no doubt from the operator, typing it in at his control console. The advantage of doing it this way is that the operating system can pass this information to *all* the different programs that are run during the day besides our sales accounting program, without them each having to obtain it individually.) But in the first version of the program, the programmer has cheated for the sake of simplicity, and loaded the values with arbitrary figures (MOVE 31 TO LAST-DAY-OF-THIS-MONTH etc.).

The values the programmer has chosen should direct the central processor to perform the INVOICE-AND-STATEMENTS procedure, which once again is just a dummy that goes through the motions. Either way, whether the central processor has had to perform INVOICE-AND-STATEMENTS or not, it finds itself forced to perform TIDY-UP, which in real life will arrange for various totals to be produced for the accountants, but here just prints a line to reassure the programmer that this simplified program is going through the right path. Then the central processor's task has finished, as it recognises by the STOP RUN instruction. It will then consult the operating system to find out what it should be doing next—perhaps a payroll—and will receive instructions from the operating system to go to the reader and demand a new program to load, and new information for the program to work on. Here are the results when the program in Fig. 10 is run, and four dummy TRANSACTIONS are given it as an exercise.

```
SET-UP PROCEDURE ENTERED
DEAL-WITH-INPUT PROCEDURE ENTERED
DEAL-WITH-INPUT PROCEDURE ENTERED
DEAL-WITH-INPUT PROCEDURE ENTERED
DEAL-WITH-INPUT PROCEDURE ENTERED
INV-AND-STATMT PROCEDURE ENTERED
TIDY-UP PROCEDURE ENTERED
```

Fig. 11 *Results of running the program in Fig. 10 on four dummy transactions: printer output*

Please follow through Fig. 10 and verify that this is what would be expected.

Now at this point some readers may be quite content to believe that the computer can obtain and store within itself electronic or magnetic representations of COMPUTE DAY-ONE-WEEK-AHEAD = TODAYS-DAY-NUMBER + 7 and, at the appropriate time, do just that. Others may well feel that while they can accept that a computer, like a pocket calculator, can deal with figures electronically, these almost English instructions could not be understood by a machine. For these readers, the mechanics of programming must be described in more detail.

How the computer circuitry responds to the programmer's instructions in quasi-English

The first thing to appreciate is that although the program is written in a language which appears at first sight like English, it is in fact very much poorer in vocabulary and more rigid in grammar. Certain command words like COMPUTE, READ, etc., are meaningful, as are arithmetic operators like + and −. Other words like TODAYS-DAY-NUMBER and SET-UP were invented by the programmer and are meaningful to him, but to the computer serve only as internal cross-references, simply equating (for example) the figure stored away in memory as a result of COMPUTE DAY-ONE-WEEK-AHEAD..., with the figure tested by IF FRIDAY THEN IF DAY-ONE-WEEK-AHEAD ... In fact if the programmer had used the word MANCHESTER-UNITED instead, the computer would have behaved exactly the same. The only difference would be that the program would be less meaningful to human beings such as the programmer himself, who in that case would have to remember that out of contrariness or misguided loyalty he used MANCHESTER-UNITED instead of DAY-ONE-WEEK-AHEAD to stand for the day one week ahead. My own weakness is to use names from J. R. R. Tolkien's works: it is nice to write CALL GANDALF (a benevolent magician) when writing part of a program dealing with awkward situations. But the allusion is lost on the computer, of course.

The program in the example is written in the computer 'language' COBOL, with its own special rules ('grammar') and set of meaningful words. But there are other languages, in which PERFORM would be meaningless except as a programmer's name for a piece of information, like MANCHESTER-UNITED, but the word CALL is significant. Besides COBOL, common used languages are FORTRAN, BASIC, ALGOL, and PL/1: each, let it be said, with their own enthusiastic followers, and with their own individual strengths and weaknesses.

Most large general purpose computers can handle any of the above languages, except that PL/1 is largely restricted to IBM computers. This raises the question, how does the computer appreciate which language its program is written in, and how does it 'understand' the program? The first question is easy enough: for a machine with an operating system the first piece of information received will specify that the program that follows is written in COBOL, FORTRAN, etc. The second is more difficult. There are computers available which are specially designed to work with one particular language, for example, BASIC, and their actual electronic circuits receive the letters and other symbols of the program and interpret and obey one instruction after another. For such machines it is impossible to make sense of programs written in another language. Such machines are called 'hard-wired, interpretive' because their understanding of the language is built into their electronics, and they 'interpret' each instruction one at a time in the original form in which they were written by the programmer, i.e. each symbol he wrote down, appears as an electronically coded symbol in its memory. Such a machine is the WANG 2200. In the jargon, we say that this machine has 'BASIC-oriented hardware'. But it is more usual for the computer not to use electronic circuits which can deal directly with a particular language, but to convert programs from the symbols used by the programmer into *different* symbols, more suited to its own workings. This conversion process is in fact normally done on the whole program in its entirety before any attempt is made to use it to carry out the job it is for. The conversion itself is a computer operation, controlled by a program, in this case called a *compiler*—for example a COBOL compiler—which has to be pre-written, usually by specialist 'software' programmers. The compiler examines groups of symbols as possible words which have a COBOL meaning like PERFORM, and treats the others as cross-references. It ends up with a translated version—one might say another program, written in a simpler language, which can be used directly. Such a scheme is a 'software compiler' approach. It is also possible to have a 'software interpretive' approach in which the original program is not converted all at one time, but left in its original form, and each instruction is converted at the time when it is due to be obeyed, not by electronic circuits, but by an 'interpretive' program. This tends to be slower than the other two approaches, but is common on computers using BASIC.

Actually some computers such as the DEC PDP11 allow BASIC programs to be run either by an interpretive program, or after compilation.

In this book we deal with the 'software compiler' method mainly, because this approach is the one used for the most part on large computer-based systems, as distinct from experimental, research, and educational computing.

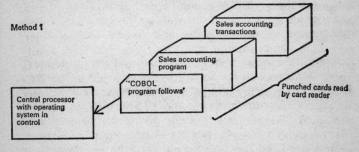

Method 1

Sales accounting transactions

Sales accounting program

"COBOL program follows"

Central processor with operating system in control

Punched cards read by card reader

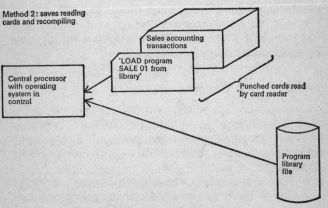

Method 2: saves reading cards and recompiling

Sales accounting transactions

'LOAD program SALE 01 from library'

Central processor with operating system in control

Punched cards read by card reader

Program library file

Fig. 12 *Loading the program*

Running the program in the computer

We have described how the central processor obtains the original program and stores it in its memory from the reader and then starts to obey it immediately. More strictly we should say that the central processor will read it, then carry out a *compilation* on it, using the operating system to supervise the work carried out by the *compiler* and possibly other programs (of interest mainly to the specialist) such as linkage editors, consolidators, and loaders. Only after this has been done without error will the operating system instruct the central processor to carry out the program. (If there *are* errors it will look for the next job to be done instead.) Now if the original program works very well and its job is to be run on the computer frequently, for example once a day, it is rather wasteful to go through the compiling process every time. For this reason the compiled program will be saved and kept on a file unit, and the useful operating system will retrieve it when all that appears in the stream of information coming from the reader is a terse reference to LOAD PROGRAM SALE01. The operating system may need some help from another program called the 'loader' to fit it into the processor's memory, but the whole operation is much faster and saves putting the program through the reader again each time it is needed.

Organisation of the Computer Department

Talking about the days when our computer system is in full working order leads us to consider the last major personnel part of the computer department: *operations*: and it is perhaps the right moment to sketch an organisation chart for the department.

We have already described the role of the systems analyst—the man or woman who can look at an existing system, envisage a new system which includes both human and

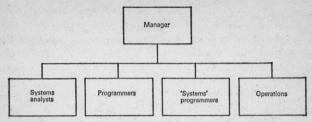

Fig. 13 *Typical computer department organisation chart*

computer sub-systems and will achieve the true objectives better, and most important, can master-mind its introduction. We have noted how the task of actually getting the computer to fulfil its part in the computer sub-system is tackled by the programmer to the systems analyst's specification. We briefly covered the need for 'systems' programmers who concentrate on making the computer easy to use by the other programmers, notably by developing, modifying, and explaining the computer's operating system for them. They may also be experts in languages, and if a programmer cannot understand why the COBOL compiler rejected his program as ungrammatical, the systems programmer will be able to help.

These three groups are largely concerned with innovation. When the new system has been designed, programmed, tested and installed, they will turn their attentions to new parts of the organisation where the computer may be able to make a contribution to the achievement of objectives. But the computer part of the installed system still needs people to operate the machinery: firstly those who are responsible for converting forms received from the human part of the system, and converting them into a medium that the computer can handle with its reader. Secondly the computer itself needs an operator to load the reader, put the right paper in the printer, make sure the customer and product files (in the example we have used) are accessible in the file

units, and so on. He or she work closely with the operating
system (a sort of human–machine combination very much
like the overall system) often communicating by means of a
typewriter: for example:

Operating system types out:
PROGRAM SALE01 LOADED,
BUT NO PRODUCT FILE ON FILE-UNIT-1.
LOAD, AND TYPE 'GO' WHEN READY.

(The operating system program, requested by SALE01
during the procedure SET-UP to OPEN the required files,
sent messages through the cables to the file-units, for them
to send back the first piece of information on the files they
contain: this information will be, by convention, the name
of the file. But none of them indicated that the product file
was there.) The human operator goes away and finds the
file in a library of files for different systems (e.g. PAYROLL,
DIVIDENDS) and puts it in the file unit. He types
GO
and the operating system tries again, finds all the files
needed, and replies:
THANKS. SALE01 STARTED
and having now OPENed the files satisfactorily, allows
SALE01 to continue with the things it has to do in SET-UP
(and they may well involve further appeals to the operating
system for help, e.g. to get today's date) and then pass on to
GET-INPUT, when the reader will come to life and start
sending signals, through the cables to the central processor,
corresponding to the contents of the CUSTOMER IN-
FORMATION, CASH RECEIPTS, and other forms we
noted earlier. The central processor alters files as appropriate and, if today is the last Friday in the month, when the
last piece of information has come in from the reader, the
printer will begin churning out invoices and statements as
lines of symbols are sent to it from the central processor.
Using our idea of expanding black boxes, we can now

indicate that the box marked 'Operations' on the chart above may contain its own organisation:

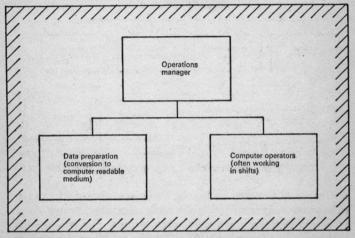

Fig. 14 *Inside the 'Operations' box in the computer department's organisation chart*

An interesting point arises here. We mentioned that the operator works closely with the computer's operating system, which is a program, and the speciality of the systems programmers. Obviously there should be a strong link between these two boxes on the organisation chart, as well as between systems programmers and application programmers. Similarly there is a link between systems analysts and application programmers, and indeed the data preparation clerks will work to rules specified by the systems analysts (see Fig. 15).

Does this invalidate the idea of independent, functional black boxes? In a sense it does: it means that contacts between boxes need not be only through the tree-like structure that represents their formal organisation. *This* structure

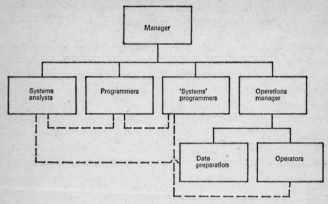

Fig. 15 *Organisation chart, plus working relationships*

corresponds perhaps to 'status': who is empowered to give salary rises or reproofs to whom. But the 'dotted line' structure represents working relationships. The two groups of people co-operate because they are suitably motivated by mutual respect for each other's contribution, or (if necessary) by being *told* to co-operate, or even by money changing hands! This last is not a reference to outright bribery, but by a method by which different parts of the same organisation offer each other services for which they make an internal charge—say £50 a day for a systems programmer to run a course on how to use the operating system for operators. This is most commonly employed between the computer department as a whole and the rest of the organisation—for example the analyst may charge his time in designing a new system to the department which is to benefit from it. Certainly it is very common for the computer's time to be charged by operations to whomever is using it: the sales accounting department, for example, when SALE01 is run. Or when programs are being tested, to the programming section, which will promptly pass the bill on to the department on whose behalf the testing is being done. There are obvious advantages in finding out the profits and losses made by the activities of the various specialists, if by so doing they are used more productively. Clearly a big firm of consultants must charge for its services in this way. But within an organisation, this method of accounting (sometimes called *re*charging) can end up an enormous administrative chore which irritates all concerned and has only a spurious efficiency. Like budgeting, operating statements, Management by Objectives and all other managerial control systems, it is no substitute for common sense, leadership, and teamwork across departmental boundaries.

Bosses and subordinates inside a program

But to return to programs made up of inter-connected black boxes, we can perhaps learn from the organisation chart of the *human* specialists in a computer department that these boxes may be linked together by lines of different kinds: the tree structure which represented managerial authority, the dotted lines, who frequently teams up with whom. In an exactly similar way we may find within a computer *program* that the black boxes may be related in a more complicated way than previously described. We could look at the 'managerial' relationships of the parts of the simple program given in Fig. 9 as in the diagram of Fig. 16:

Each black box below the level of the first two has one, and only one, 'manager' box to tell it to 'perform'. Vertical line connections indicate subordination. But supposing we have some extremely useful black box which could provide a service to more than one 'manager' box?

For example, we shall need to find the Large Teapot product information when, during the DEAL-WITH-INPUT procedure, there is an amendment of price from 50p to 55p, and again during INVOICE-AND-STATEMENTS when we are billing Mrs. Thomas for a large teapot,

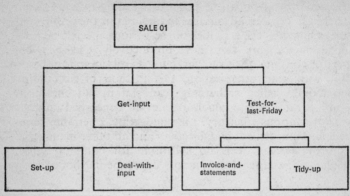

Fig. 16 *'Managerial' structure of program*

and need to refer to the latest price. The business of finding the Large Teapot information in the product file is not going to be trivially easy: it is akin to the problem faced by a human clerk when faced with a large filing cabinet, and we shall have to work out a systematic way of choosing the 'drawers' to try, and then searching the 'suspended pockets', to recover the information quickly and efficiently. More will be said about this soon. So we will very likely think in terms of a black box called FIND-ORDER-INF to do the job, and this will be invoked in two places in the program: it will have, so to speak, two managers empowered to tell it to perform. We *could* have given them a copy of the black box each, one called (say) FIND-ORDER-INF-A and the other FIND-ORDER-INF-B, with identical contents, but this would make the program unnecessarily long.

But the slave-with-two-masters approach is neater (see Fig. 17).

The idea of a general purpose procedure, used in several places, is one of the most powerful concepts of computing. A common name for such a procedure is a *sub-routine*, which conveys the notion of subordination.

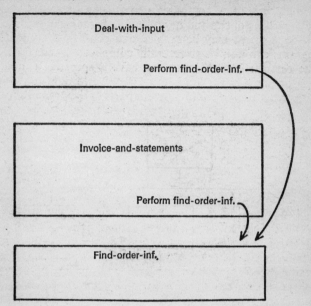

Fig. 17 *A procedure offering a service to several others*

So in our original hierarchical chart Fig. 16 we now have to draw in the sub-routine FIND-ORDER-INF with lines showing it is subordinate to SALE01 but employed at different times by two other procedures. See Fig. 18.

Fortunately in the program we are discussing it can only be called on to PERFORM by one or other of its 'employers' at any one time, so we avoid the problems that human subordinates have when they have more than one person telling them what to do.

Later we shall look at situations where this *can* happen inside the computer, so that the same sub-routine *is* being used by two different 'employers' at the same time: or even where a sub-routine can be used by itself. It is some comfort for members of a computer department to reflect that, although the politics and organisational complexity of their own department may be tangled and confusing, computer programs can also be structurally complicated, and for the same reason: in both cases we have a specialist (human being or procedure) who is too expensive to duplicate, but whose skills are needed in different parts of the organisation.

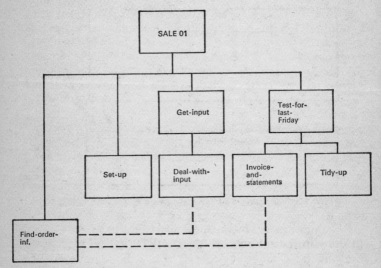

Fig. 18 *Amended 'managerial' program structure*

Computer-readable media—punched cards, paper tape, etc.

We will conclude this chapter with a review of the actual hardware which underlies all the rather generalised expressions like 'file-unit', 'reader' and 'conversion of human documents to a medium which the computer reader can handle'. We deliberately avoided getting involved in the physical nature of these machines because we were interested only in their functional contribution to the computer-based system as a whole. However, now we know the 'why', the 'what' will be more intelligible. Each machine is termed a 'peripheral' part of the computer, in contrast to the central processor.

If we have a symbol, such as the letter L in LOBSTER POT, written by someone on a document, and if the computer is to do something with this L (e.g. transfer it, and OBSTER POT as well, on to the top of an invoice) this symbol must be translated into the electronic or magnetic equivalent symbol which the electronic circuits of the computer can handle. The most usual way to do this is to pass the document to a card punch operator who reads the document, and presses keys like typewriter keys, symbol by symbol. As he or she does this, holes are punched in a post-card-sized card, which typically takes 80 symbols—letters, figures, spaces, etc. As an example, the program in Fig. 10 was initially written on a form, then passed for punching: one card was punched per line (which means a certain amount of wastage when less than 80 symbols are present). The particular card punch was able to print the symbols along the top, so that human beings could read them too. Here is an example:

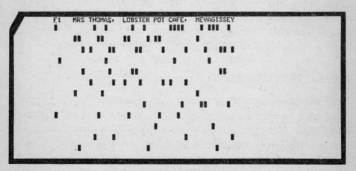

Fig. 19 *Punched card*

The whole TRANS-FILE when punched, makes up a *pack*, or (American) *deck* of cards, one per line. The symbol used in systems design for such a pack of cards is:

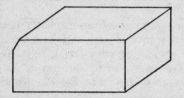

Fig. 20 *Symbol for a pack of cards*

A pack of these cards is placed in the *hopper* of a *card reader* connected by cable to the central processor, which signals it, via the cable, to extract the first card and pass it over a metal roller while pressing 80 metal brushes on it from the other side. Each brush covers one possible symbol, and the times during the passage of the card when a particular brush makes electrical contact through to the roller, indicate the position of the hole or holes. So we have 80 wires registering electrical signals, which can be transmitted back through the cable to the central processor, which can electronically carry out any transformations on them into whatever symbolism it works most conveniently with, and can then place them in its memory ready to be worked on. All this process is triggered by the instruction READ TRANS-FILE in the program: as a result, the FORM-RECORD will contain 80 symbols known collectively as FORM-INF (see Fig. 10). The other instructions in the program will be followed and the program causes the central processor to GO TO GET-INPUT, when it once again sends a signal to the reader for the next card, and so on, until the reader replies with a signal effectively saying 'no more cards, I'm afraid', which will be interpreted by the central computer so as to cause the AT END action to be followed.

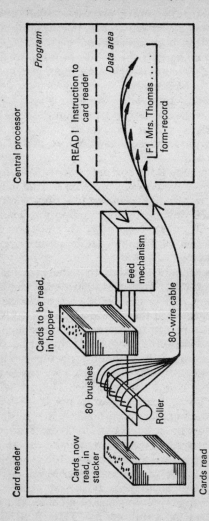

Fig. 21 Schematic of card reader and central processor (card readers can operate at speeds typically between 100 and 1000 cards per minute)

It should be noted that the central processor usually operates so fast that it would spend most of its time waiting for the card reader to give it more information, even at 1000 cards per minute. Early computers solved this problem by having small computers devoted to copying information from cards to *magnetic tape* (to be described shortly) which can be read much faster. Nowadays the *same* computer is used for both tasks: part of it will be running a program, say B, which involves calculations and references to files, and which obtains its input from a magnetic tape or disc, and places its results—lines of output—similarly on to magnetic tape or disc files. While running B the computer *also* runs a program copying the results of the *previous* program A from magnetic tape or disc on to the line printer, and runs a program reading cards and copying the information in them on to magnetic tape or disc for the *next* job, C. This overlapping technique is termed 'off-lining' (ICL terminology) or 'SPOOLing' (IBM).

You will have probably noticed that the card for Mrs. Thomas had a prefix F1. This might have been almost any other suitable code, and is used simply to enable the computer system to check that the information received is from a particular form type—in this case a customer name and address form. Otherwise the program might not be able to tell that the form was in fact about a customer. Without being given the very complex rules which we use to make these distinctions, it could well take Mrs. Thomas as being a *product*, like a Large Teapot. (Let us not laugh and say that only a stupid computer could make such a mistake. It *is* possible to program a computer to avoid such errors provided we can analyse exactly what distinguishes the class of products from the class of customers, for example, the occurrence of the string of symbols MR. MRS. MISS or ESQ., could indicate customers. It is just cheaper and quicker to tell it explicitly by means of a code. And might not a human clerk be confused by 'THE PORRIDGE

BOWL, WORCESTER'? and not know whether it was a product or a customer?)

Besides punched cards there are several other ways in which information can be communicated from human beings to computers:

Punched paper tape. This is prepared in a similar way but is presented to the computer reader as a roll of punched tape which is read by being pulled over a row of photocells which send typically eight 'hole/no hole' signals back to the central processor for each symbol. A typical speed for a reader is 1000 symbols per second, when limited by the mechanics of the reader itself rather than the rate at which the central processor issues READ instructions.

Character recognition. It is possible to put the original human-produced documents into a machine which scans them for printed or written symbols, or for marks like ticks against printed boxes, and is able to 'recognise' what symbol is meant. It is most reliable when the symbols are printed by machine, and least reliable when attempting to interpret human handwriting. Such devices are used for reading cheques, electricity meter cards, etc. (see Chapter 4). A typical speed is 2000 symbols per second.

Direct keying in. We saw how the computer operator could have a dialogue with the operating system by typing at a special console connected to the central processor. It is perfectly possible to use this typewriter rather than the reader to put in other information such as 'MRS THOMAS . . .' or an actual program, but the computer would be slowed up to the speed of the human typing rate, which is much less than the rates quoted above. Some small computers like accounting machines or scientific desk-top computers accept this but no operations manager will allow a computer, costing perhaps £200 an hour, to be idle most of the time between successive key-strokes of a human being! However it is possible for the computer to deal with *many* typewriter operators all typing together, by effectively taking the electrical signals from the keyboard to the central processor and simultaneously assembling the symbols in their appropriate slots in its memory. In this way the combined rate of character transmission may be high enough to match the computer's appetite for data.

This raises a new problem, the solution to which is important to many other situations. We saw how a program might contain an instruction like:

READ TRANS-FILE

where TRANS-FILE contains FORM-RECORDS each of 80 symbols (known collectively as FORM-INF in our program).

The central processor had to stop until all 80 symbols (or 'characters') had been moved from the reader to the area of memory known to our program as FORM-INF. If they had to be typed, there could be several seconds delay: expensive to a £200/hour machine! We avoided this by converting the forms away from the computer into a form such as punched cards which the computer can accept quickly. We also noted that the techniques of 'off-lining' or 'SPOOLing' improve efficiency still further. However, these techniques inevitably lengthen the time between the submission of information to the computer, and its response. What about systems, like airline reservations, where rapid response is essential?

Supposing we attached ten, slow, human-speed typewriters, and the average input rate was thus increased to a level which more nearly matched the computer's speed of processing. The situation might be represented by the arrangement in Fig. 22:

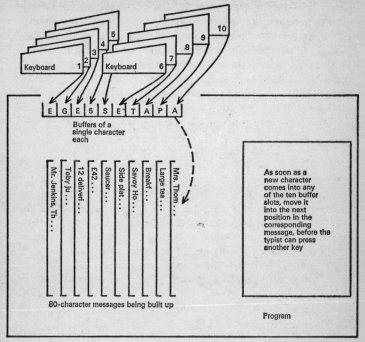

Fig. 22 *Computer accepting 10 messages from each of 10 typists*

A digression on how to arrange for a computer to handle information coming in from several peripherals at once

What is wanted is some means by which the central processor can send a signal to each of say ten typewriters asking for a symbol (or 'character') in the typist's own good time, and to arrange for the character to be placed in a slot or '*buffer*' in memory when it arrives. But there must also be some sort of indicator set to show that the buffer has been filled, so that the central processor can transfer the single character out of the buffer for that typewriter and into the space in a larger area reserved for the building up of the whole message, *before* the typist gets round to pressing the next key (otherwise the first character in the buffer would be lost for ever as the new one comes in on top).

After doing this the central processor should see whether the message area is now full (and if so ignore this typewriter henceforth), otherwise signal the typewriter to send another character. When all the message areas are full the program can stop. The program block diagram for this could be that of Fig. 23:

This logic block diagram is more complicated than Fig. 7 and will repay a little study. The boxes joined on by dotted lines contain comments.

The reader may think that we are going into rather great detail on this topic of direct keying in as a means of input. The reason is not only that this method of getting information into a computer is gaining ground over other methods, but that the technical problem of programming it is of interest and involves concepts which are used in very many other computer situations. A basic one introduced in the block diagram is the idea of looping, i.e. repeating a sequence of instructions a controlled number of times. We have Fig. 24(a) instead of (b).

We may also note that the same procedure

	CALL FOR A CHARACTER FROM A TYPEWRITER (I)	

is used in another place later on in the program: an example of a 'black box' having two 'managers' who both make use of its services.

Another point of interest is the use of *buffers* into which information is placed in the central processor's memory on arrival (by cable) from another source. The program has the

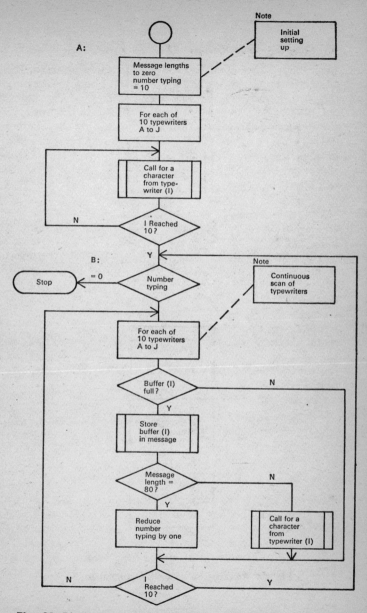

Fig. 23 *Block diagram of logic to build up 10 messages of 80 characters from 10 typewriters all being used at once*

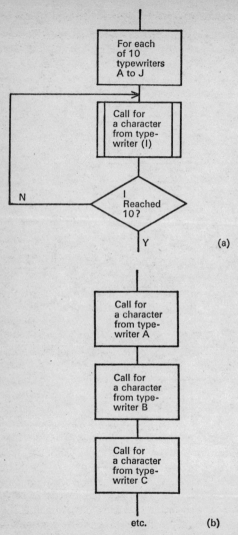

Fig. 24 *Repeating a series of instructions*

responsibility for copying the contents of these buffers into message areas before they are needed again to receive the next character. This goes with the idea that the central processor can be getting on with other work between the time it sends a signal asking for information, and the information actually arriving: it is like a juggler tossing a ball into the air and catching and tossing several others before the first one comes down. To gain some appreciation of the speed at which the computer operates, during the fifth of a second or so between successive strokes by a typist, a large computer could carry out some 100 000 additions of 10 digit numbers.

The programs to deal with multiple typewriters and similar situations are not usually done by the same kind of *application* programmer who would program the sales accounting system we took as an example earlier. It is more likely to be incorporated as a service carried out by the operating system—so that the application programmer can use the service as a 'black box' which presents him with complete lines of information from the typewriters when he requests them. Moreover much of the work of 'handling peripherals', to drop into the jargon, is today performed by subsidiary 'mini-computers' or even 'micro-computers' which do much of the task of buffer filling and emptying and testing on behalf of the operating system, which regards *them* as black boxes! And such machines often operate, not so much by scanning, but by a system of 'interrupts', by which a typewriter does not wait to be asked to send information, but forces the processor to leave whatever processing it is doing, and enter a special section of program devoted to accepting the character whose arrival triggered the interruption, after which it can resume its previous activity. We may consider all these techniques as means by which the central processor can handle information which comes in *asynchronously*, i.e. at times of the sender's choosing, not at the central processor's request. This is essential for many applications like monitoring nuclear reactors or airline reservations.

A further digression on the choice of language for programming problems: a PL/1 example

Lastly we can use 'direct keying in' and the technical problems in programming for it as a reason to say something more about programming languages. The language COBOL is widely used for problems which can be described in narrative appropriate to a description of a human clerical task: READ TRANS-FILE AT END PERFORM TEST-FOR-LAST-FRIDAY is rather stilted, but could conceivably be an instruction to a human clerk. But in many cases we need to make the central processor do things which human clerks do not do, like doing ten jobs at once, or calculating space-craft velocities to fifteen places of decimals. Hence COBOL is not often used for such tasks. It is possible to write programs in a language very close indeed to the language used by the electronic circuitry of the machine, in which case the programs turn out to make good use of whatever features the computer may have. The program is then very hard to understand for a layman, but then he probably would not appreciate even the purpose of the program. Such languages are termed 'low-level', e.g. Assembler, PLAN. Alternatively, where the bias is towards scientific or mathematical problems, the languages FORTRAN or ALGOL are easy to follow by scientists and mathematicians. (Even human beings have *technical* languages they use in particular situations, whether in medicine, accountancy or golf, when normal English is longwinded or imprecise.)

One or two languages attempt to allow the programmer to control the computer right down to the basic circuitry level, and at the same time be understandable. CORAL, JOVIAL and PL/1 are in this category, and for interest a PL/1 program to carry out the 10 typewriter problem is given below (Fig. 25).

```pli
A:      PROC OPTIONS(MAIN);
/********************* SET UP AND INITIALIZE BUFFERS ETC ***/
        DECLARE BUFFER(10) CHARACTER(1);
        DECLARE MESSAGE(10) CHARACTER(80);
        DECLARE BUFFERFULL(10) EVENT;
        DECLARE MESSAGELENGTH(10) INITIAL ( (10) 0 );
        DECLARE NUMBERTYPING INITIAL (10);
/********************* CALL FOR A CHARACTER FROM EACH T/W ****/
        DO I = 1 TO 10;
        CALL STARTREAD(I);
        END;
/********************* KEEP SCANNING UNTIL ALL FINISHED ******
B:      DO WHILE(NUMBERTYPING > 0);
        DO I = 1 TO 10;
        IF ( COMPLETION(BUFFERFULL(I)) ) THEN DO;
        CALL STOREBUFFER(I);
        IF (MESSAGELENGTH(I) < 80) THEN CALL STARTREAD(I);
        ELSE NUMBERTYPING=NUMBERTYPING − 1;
        END;    /*  OF ACTION WHEN BUFFERFULL  */
        END;    /*  OF ONE SCAN ROUND THE 10 TYPEWRITERS  */
        END;    /*  OF PERIOD WHEN ANYBODY IS TYPING  */
        GO TO C;    /*  NUMBERTYPING NOW ZERO, END OF RUN  */
/********************* PROCEDURES USED BY ABOVE PROGRAM *******/
/********************* GET A CHARACTER FROM TYPEWRITER ( I )  */
STARTREAD:  PROC(I);
        DECLARE CHOICE(10) LABEL;
        GO TO CHOICE(I);
CHOICE( 1): READ FILE(TYPEA) INTO (BUFFER( 1)) EVENT(BUFFERFULL( 1));
            RETURN;
CHOICE( 2): READ FILE(TYPEB) INTO (BUFFER( 2)) EVENT(BUFFERFULL( 2));
            RETURN;
CHOICE( 3): READ FILE(TYPEC) INTO (BUFFER( 3)) EVENT(BUFFERFULL( 3));
            RETURN;
CHOICE( 4): READ FILE(TYPED) INTO (BUFFER( 4)) EVENT(BUFFERFULL( 4));
            RETURN;
CHOICE( 5): READ FILE(TYPEE) INTO (BUFFER( 5)) EVENT(BUFFERFULL( 5));
            RETURN;
CHOICE( 6): READ FILE(TYPEF) INTO (BUFFER( 6)) EVENT(BUFFERFULL( 6));
            RETURN;
CHOICE( 7): READ FILE(TYPEG) INTO (BUFFER( 7)) EVENT(BUFFERFULL( 7));
            RETURN;
CHOICE( 8): READ FILE(TYPEI) INTO (BUFFER( 8)) EVENT(BUFFERFULL( 8));
            RETURN;
CHOICE( 9): READ FILE(TYPEJ) INTO (BUFFER( 9)) EVENT(BUFFERFULL( 9));
            RETURN;
CHOICE(10): READ FILE(TYPEK) INTO (BUFFER(10)) EVENT(BUFFERFULL(10));
            RETURN;
        END;
/********************* MOVE THE CHARACTER INTO THE MESSAGE  **/
STOREBUFFER:  PROC(I);
        MESSAGELENGTH(I)=MESSAGELENGTH(I) + 1;
        SUBSTR(MESSAGE(I),MESSAGELENGTH(I),1) = BUFFER(I);
        END;
/********************* END OF THE COMPLETE OPERATION *********/
C:      END A;
```

Fig. 25 Program in PL/1 to build up ten messages of 80 characters coming from 10 typewriters

A number of differences from COBOL are apparent:

> There is no DATA division, but values can be DE-CLARED. For example, a name BUFFERFULL can be associated with an event—in this case, the completion of a character transfer into a buffer.
>
> Comments can be added within /* and */
>
> A group of instructions can be defined by DO . . . and . . . END
>
> CALL is used instead of PERFORM, and a value can be passed to the procedure being used as a 'black box' performing a service, inside brackets.

> PL/1 requires the programmer to use brackets rather often. This is because the language is more flexible than COBOL, and the interpretation of an instruction can be ambiguous if brackets are left out.

> When a READ is carried out, the central processor need not stop until the information transfer has been completed, as in the COBOL example: it can go on, and can discover (IF (COMPLETION . . .)) whether the information has arrived by examining whether an associated EVENT has happened.

> The language is obviously less like normal English than the COBOL example earlier. We use the abbreviation > instead of 'IS GREATER THAN', for example.

> PL/1 provides some dodges which programmers like, such as SUBSTR a little lower down, which lets a programmer specify that the central processor is to insert a substring of characters into a larger string: in this case a single character into the message area at a point defined by MESSAGELENGTH for the particular typewriter under consideration in the scan.

This is not a programming book and no harm will be done if you look at this example and just take on trust that it does what the 10 typewriter problem demanded, and in the chapters that follow on specific computer applications, are happy that some of the extraordinary feats they perform are simply extensions of these basic concepts. But if you feel like mulling over it and cross-referencing it to Fig. 23, the block diagram, until it makes complete sense, you may be the kind of person who should take up the programmer's art.

Remote terminals

After this long digression prompted by the implications of direct keying in as an input method, we will mention one or two others fairly briefly. *Remote terminals* are of two kinds, *batch* terminals which are just like the card readers or paper tape readers already described, but connected to the computer by telephone lines rather than by local cables, and slower *keyboard* terminals similarly connected, which are like the typewriters discussed above. The commonest kind is the Teletype, for which most computer professionals have an affection because of its low cost and reliability during long night sessions communicating with a distant computer. Other terminals have a television-style screen instead of paper.

Computer people sometimes talk about 'idiot' terminals and 'intelligent' (or, American, 'smart') terminals. The latter have a certain amount of electronic circuitry, even going so far as a mini-computer and memory, included in them. This makes it possible for the terminal itself to process information without troubling the distant main computer. An analyst might, for example, find it most economic for the terminal to have a small PRODUCT file which it could use to check deliveries and prices, but have the CUSTOMER file on the main computer (or vice versa). In this way the telephone bills and main computer time might be reduced. The extreme case of an intelligent terminal is the attachment of another large computer: in this case the 'terminal' may deal with all problems except one or two which are passed to its associate, either because it has not got the capacity to handle so large a problem, or because the other computer acts as a summarising and controlling unit. Subordinates may be just as intelligent as their managers! A symbolic representation of some possibilities is shown below:

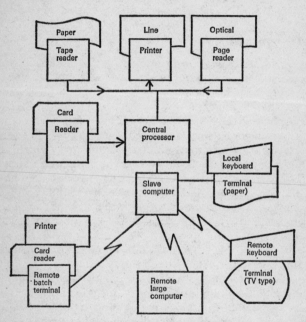

Fig. 26 *A computer with local peripherals, including a slave computer connected to distant terminals and another large computer*

Big computers called on to tackle big problems are known colloquially as *number crunchers*. At Brunel University the Computer Unit owns a small Modular 1 computer which is loaded with a program for reading punched cards, printing lines, and sending and receiving messages over a telephone line to the University of London computer centre's Control Data computer, whose own programs accept and transmit messages. As a matter of fact the Modular 1 program is designed to deal with messages in the same format as the ULCC computer would 'expect' if it was connected to a remote batch terminal supplied by Control Data. Similarly the Modular 1 can be loaded with a program which can make it 'seem' like an IBM remote batch terminal (IBM 2780) or IBM small computer used as a terminal (IBM 1130) to the University College big IBM System/360. So it is convenient to use a real computer as a terminal since it can be attached to several different makes of big computer.

Storing information within the computer

All the peripheral devices mentioned above are used to transfer symbols or characters like 1, 2, Q, + to and from the central processor. Later we shall come across devices which can pick up temperatures, brain waves, sounds, etc., and symbolise them for the central processor, and conversely take symbols from the central processor and use them to draw pictures, fire rockets, etc. But there is another class of peripheral device to consider—the 'file-units' which we proposed to use for the storage of bulk information. One might wonder why we cannot just use the central processor's memory for this purpose. Any symbol (or group of symbols like 'MRS. THOMAS' or '31', can be stored conveniently there, and can be referred to by a suitable name in the program (like CUSTOMER-NAME or NUMBER-OF-DAYS-THIS-MONTH). The information can be stored or recovered for processing in millionths of a second. However, this kind of storage is expensive. The cost of the memory to store 10 000 customer names of up to 80 characters long, and all the other information about the customer (address, invoices outstanding, etc.) amounting say to a total of 400 characters each, i.e. four million characters in total, could cost in the region of a million pounds or more. Obviously this is out of the question. We need to have *some* of this fast expensive memory for the central processor to use for program, operating system, buffers, and working storage, but the Product File and Customer File must be stored in a cheaper medium. Two main kinds of storage device are available: magnetic tape and magnetic discs.

Magnetic tape
A reel of tape 2400 feet long costs about twenty pounds and can store about twenty million characters, i.e. only a ten thousandth of a penny per character. However, we need a tape drive to pass the tape over a read/write head according to instructions from the central processor:

● 'Read characters and transfer them through the cable to specified positions in memory'
● 'Write' (as above, *from* memory to tape)
● 'Rewind'

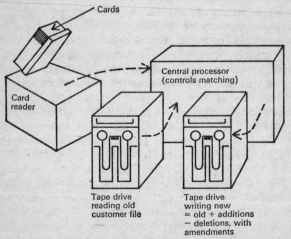

Fig. 27 *Computer with tape drives*

Fig. 28 *IBM 8420 Magnetic Tape Subsystem*

This tape drive will cost about twenty thousand pounds with the electronics to connect it up. Usually we will use tape drives in pairs, one reading the current version of a file, the other making a fresh copy of it with any amendments, additions or deletions which the central processor program actions on the authority of information coming in from the reader. The fresh copy is then used on the next run, the old copy is 'scratched'—jargon, meaning that the tape reel can be over-written with new information. The tape drive itself will, in the course of a day, read or write tapes for many

Conditions

Conditions	1	2	3	4	5	6	7	8	9	10	11
									Higher	Same	Lower
Start of run	Y	N									
Customer number on tape record last read into memory, is greater than one before	—	N	Y i.e. correct ascending sequence			N i.e. correct ascending (or same) sequence			N		
Customer number on card information last read into memory, is less than one before	—	—									
Attempt to read a tape record when END of tape reached	—	—	—	Y	—	—	—	—	N		
Attempt to read a card when END reached	—	—	—	—	Y	—	—	—	N		
Tape customer number in memory = 999999	—	—	—	—	—	Y	Y	—	N		
Card customer number in memory = 999999	—	—	—	—	—	Y	N	Y	N		
Customer number of tape record in memory compared with that of card information	—	—	—	—	—	—	—	—	Higher	Same	Lower

Actions	1	2	3	4	5	6	7	8	9	10	11
Create new customer record in memory: card is for a new customer									✓		
Write customer record in memory to new tape, unless marked for removal							✓	✓			✓
Alter customer record in memory according to card information or mark for removal if Deletion										✓	
Stop run. Rewind tapes		✓	✓			✓					
Error detected: bad sequence		✓	✓								
Read a card into memory	✓						✓		✓	✓	
Read a tape record into memory	✓							✓			✓
Put a dummy customer tape record in memory with customer number = 999999				✓							
Put a dummy card in memory with customer number = 999999 (bigger than any possible *real* number)					✓						

Fig. 29 *Decision table: logic for sequential processing of a customer file on magnetic tape with amendments, additions, and deletions specified by form information on cards*

different systems: sales, payroll, etc., etc. An important point about magnetic tape is that information on it has to be extracted *serially*: usually it is grouped in *records* corresponding to some logical grouping of information, such as all the particulars about the LOBSTER POT CAFÉ, but if this record is near the end of the tape, it will take a minute or two to reach it (as against a millionth of a second or two for information in memory).

The way in which a program can marry up records held on tape, with amendments, deletions, and additions coming in on cards, *provided both streams are in the same order*, can be expressed conveniently in yet another documentary layout, a 'decision table' (see Fig. 29).

It is likely that a programmer would use such a decision table as a specification for writing his program, and when he had written it, would trace through the path of instructions followed in each combination of *conditions*, to ensure that the path included all the *actions* prescribed by the corresponding *rule*. There are also ways of using the decision table more directly: we could punch cards with its contents coded on them, and apply a special compiler which will convert the table into a working program.

In fact there is a whole class of programming languages called 'table-driven' as contrasted with 'procedural' ones as described so far, which includes decision table processors, and report program generators.

Magnetic discs (American: 'disks')
A drawback of magnetic tape for music is that if you just want to play one movement in a symphony, you have to run the tape through any preceding movements. With a record, however, you can work out which grooves correspond to the movement wanted, and move the stylus across to the right position. Similarly if we wanted the record for MRS. THOMAS on *tape* we should have to go through MR. ABSOLOM, etc. first.

If at the time we did this we were only interested in one or two of MRS. THOMAS' predecessors on the file, or if we were in a hurry to obtain MRS. THOMAS' particulars (she might be on the 'phone complaining she had been charged twice for her Large Teapot), then the magnetic tape file is clumsy and would waste not only MRS. THOMAS' time, but the time of the computer itself which could be charged at £200 per hour.

Accordingly the systems analyst might decide that the customer records should be stored on a file unit more like a gramophone—a disc drive. Information is stored as records on circular (not spiral) tracks, with typically twenty records of 400 characters on each, and 200 tracks per disc surface, of which there are typically twenty also. Hence the total capacity of the disc drive would be:

$$400 \times 20 \times 200 \times 20 = 32\ 000\ 000 \text{ characters,}$$

which is roughly enough to store the letters, figures, and spaces in the texts of 80 books of this size. The EDS-100 shown in Fig. 30 actually holds up to 100 million characters.

The cost of a disc pack is about £200, i.e. cost per character stored is around one thousandth of a penny: dearer than magnetic tape but much cheaper than memory. The disc drive is also more expensive than a tape unit.

The discs are mounted as an assembly on a spindle: typically 11 discs are used to provide 20 recording surfaces (the exposed surfaces of the top and bottom discs are not used).

The assembly can be moved about safely under a locking cover with a handle, which is removed when the assembly is mounted in the drive ready to be used.

When the assembly ('disc-pack') is in position in the drive, 20 read/write heads, one for each surface, and mounted on a 'comb' move inwards so that each is aligned with one of the 200 tracks on its recording surface: all heads are on the corresponding track, of course (see Fig. 31).

Fig. 30 *ICL EDS–100 disc drive*

If we know that MRS. THOMAS' information is on the underside of the second from the top disc, in track 87 out from the centre, we need to

(a) Mount the disc-pack if not already mounted,
(b) Get the central processor to obey a SEEK instruction which causes it to send a signal to the drive, to move the comb to the 87th track position,

(c)   Get it to signal the drive to select output from the third head,

(d)   Get it to scan until MRS. THOMAS' record comes round (like a child on a roundabout) and has been identified by some code,

(e)   Send the information following the code down the cable to be stored in memory.

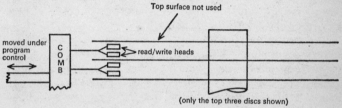

(only the top three discs shown)

Fig. 31 *Side view of disc and access mechanism*

Of these operations, the first takes a minute or two, and the analyst would try to design the system so that when MRS. THOMAS' (or anyone else's information) is needed, the CUSTOMER FILE disc-pack is mounted on a drive. To avoid having an expensive drive tied up on this job at times when few enquiries might arise, he may specify definite periods during which enquiries are allowed, and others when they are not, at which time the drive could be used to hold the disc-pack for payroll records, for example. The analyst will weigh the minor inconvenience of not being able to get at MRS. THOMAS' record at midnight with the waste of equipment.

The comb movement takes only a fraction of a second (e.g. 50 thousandths) to position itself over the right tracks, but this varies with the distance to go. Head selection is electronic and takes a negligible time. The time taken for the discs to rotate an average of half a revolution before the required record comes up, is around 10 thousandths of a second. Lastly, the time to transfer all MRS. THOMAS' information to memory depends on how much there is of it, but 400 characters will take around one thousandth of a second.

The total time to place the record in memory where the processor can work on it is thus a fraction of a second if the disc-pack is already mounted. But what has not been discussed is *how* the processor is able to give the right instructions (move to the *87th* track, etc.) to locate the record, having been given from some typewriter or punched card a key like 'THOMAS' or '1286-34/B'.

The procedure for finding the record is very much like that of a human clerk faced with finding a record in a filing cabinet: which drawer? which pocket? Like him, the program may use *indices* which give a list of keys and the location of the corresponding record, and these indices themselves may be stored on a disc pack (just as a list of paper records is itself a paper record). Accordingly the procedure to find MRS. THOMAS may be a little longer and more complicated than at first sight.

If, as a result of the incoming information, MRS. THOMAS' record should be changed (e.g. a credit allowed on the teapot billed twice in error), exactly the same procedure can be followed: the read/write head transfers the original record, plus alterations carried out by the program, e.g. SUBTRACT CREDIT FROM BALANCE-OWING back into its old place on the track, over-writing what was there before. If a new customer is added, the indices must also be amended. There is always a lurking danger with this technique (jargon: 'update-in-place') that something will go wrong and nonsense will be written on the disc-pack, e.g. if there is a power fluctuation, or a program error. In this case, the old information has been lost, whereas in magnetic *tape* processing the old tape is not re-used until the new tape has been checked. To ensure that important information is not lost, the systems analyst may well specify that the computer procedures must include a *security dump* at intervals—effectively, the taking of a copy of the disc-pack, record by record, simply in case it gets damaged. This requirement also increases the cost of disc processing.

However, most modern computers use discs extensively for files for the reasons given above, and magnetic tapes largely as ancillaries. Discs are also useful for holding the programs themselves—the operating system, told by a single card to run the SALE01 program, reads it from disc into memory, then allows it to take control. Such a process is very much faster than reading the program from cards as originally described. The complexities of searching indices and moving the heads to the right track can be delegated to the operating system program to some extent: the programmer can write:

READ (file name, etc.)
KEY (e.g. '1028' or even 'MRS. THOMAS')

and the instruction will be broken down into several steps:

(a) Move heads to index area on disc-pack A and read index
(b) Scan index for '1028'
(c) If not found, read more index, or if end of index, take 'NOT FOUND' action
(d) When found, pick up corresponding record location indicator, move heads to right area on main file disc-pack and read record. Check '1028' in the record
(e) Return control to the program.

Summary

In this chapter we have covered a great deal of ground: we have started with an imaginary sales accounting system, and showed how the *people* involved have to be considered first, and how the systems analyst tackles the problem. We saw how the programmer is called upon to arrange for the computer part of the system to make its contribution, by setting up the central processor to carry out the necessary instructions, which control the peripheral readers, printers, or terminals, or which operate on information placed within the central processor's own memory. We saw how even the overall structure of the computer's task in this system can be written as a simplified program in COBOL, ready for elaboration as details of processing are specified by the systems analyst. Then we looked at the organisation of the people in a typical computer department who work together to develop and run a system—and this prompted a comparison between organisational hierarchies and systems.

The practicalities of getting information into and out of a computer led to notes on readers, printers, and more exotic devices, and direct keying in in turn led on to discussions about programs to handle multiple peripherals, and an example in another language, PL/1.

Lastly we looked at devices for storing large volumes of information—magnetic tape and disc drives—more economically than within central processor memory.

3

Computer-based Systems Categorised by Speed of Response. Slow-response Systems

The last chapter gave the minimum technical background information about the functions of computer people, equipment, and programs needed to understand the systems they support. Now it is time to look at these systems themselves.

There are several ways in which we could organise this review: we could categorise computer-based systems by type of industry, or even by alphabetic order or organisation name. But a major purpose of the review is to show how important *time* is in our subject-matter, and so the systems have been described roughly in order of *response speed*: from the slowest to the fastest. As we saw in the section on storage, the faster you want a piece of information, the more the system costs. On the other hand, the overall system may meet its objectives better if information can be extracted from files and actioned rapidly: indeed it may be quite useless if a certain minimum response time is not achieved, as, for example, a computer-based system for landing a spacecraft: it might well hit the ground before the computer has calculated how much thrust to apply in order to slow its descent.

The economics of response time

We can see the relationship between response time and benefits from the following example. Suppose we wish to set up a 'journey planning' system which will enable people to telephone a central office where clerks will tell them which buses, trains, etc. they should take to get from one place to another, and rather than giving the clerks printed time-tables, we provide computer terminals with typewriter-style keyboards so that they can enter the points of origin and destination, and desired arrival time and date, and get back from a computer a suggested best sequence of transport—'a 138 bus to Victoria, then the 10.35 to Brighton, etc.'

We could draw a graph of the expected benefits of the system, set against expected cost, for various levels of service, i.e. by the response time which has to elapse between the enquirer telephoning and his getting an answer (see Fig. 32).

We can see that a system which takes several days to answer will still cost money but will not attract any enquirers. One or two people who plan well in advance will perhaps use the system if it takes a day to respond, but there will be extra costs because the clerks have to ring back with the answers.

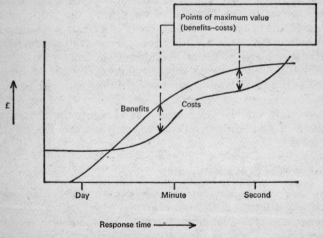

Fig. 32 *Relationship between a system's response time and value = 'journey planning' system*

The system really becomes popular when people can ring up on the spur of the moment and have their journey planned for them within a few minutes. Moreover the system can give a better answer because the latest traffic jams, breakdowns, and extra services can be taken account of. However, this improvement costs money, and at about a minute's response time it may well be that a more advanced type of computer or programming approach will be necessary —so that there will be a steep rise in costs. But after this point the curve flattens again and a second 'maximum value point' occurs when the response time is a few seconds: the computer can cope, the enquirer is impressed with the service he is getting, and the clerk can deal with one enquirer at a time, not waiting for the computer, or alternatively getting muddled trying to deal with several enquiries at once to avoid idle time.

Beyond this point computer costs begin to rise steeply (an infinitely quick response will always be infinitely expensive) but the additional benefit to the enquirer and the clerk will not be significant.

If a systems analyst had prepared such a graph, which is likely to be different for different systems, he will be able to recommend what response time should be aimed at and hence the type of computer and programming approach, and volume of business to expect. If he is cautious he may well suggest a system to fit the first maximum value point, which has the advantage of lower outlay at risk and a higher percentage of benefits: however, there might be good reasons for being bold and aiming at the second level. The best compromise may well be a design which can deal with the first level but is easily developed to cope with the second, i.e. trying to flatten out the costs line to make the system less critical and more flexible to cope with different volumes of business.

Although we have spoken in terms of money, there are many systems in which the benefits cannot be expressed in money terms—medical systems, or defence. Nevertheless, it is essential to express the benefits in *some* precise form (probability of patient being given correct treatment, or of intercepting an enemy missile) so that it is clear just what we are proposing to spend and what we shall get from it. It is largely a political or social decision, whether to spend a thousand pounds on raising the probability of Mrs. Jones recovering from a broken hip by .1 or on reducing the chances of a missile reaching London by .001. But the analyst should enable such choices to be expressed in these clear terms when presenting his recommendations to those who hold the purse-strings. This idea of cost/benefit analysis was applied by Robert MacNamara during his time as US Secretary of Defense.

Incidentally a system for planning journeys is not an imaginary idea. Burroughs, a major computer manufacturer, offer a program free of charge to help any group of employees plan the pooling of cars to go to work. Since going to work is a regular journey, the benefits of the system are secured even if it is run infrequently and therefore, at minimum cost. In the USA, the major car rental companies use computers to plan how they should re-position vehicles to meet demand. Avis' computer system is called Wizard, and, since its function is also to issue paperwork for car hirers anxious to be on their way, is a *rapid*-response system. However, no system has yet been produced which has information on all forms of transport available—road, rail, air and sea. The difficulty is not a technical one, but that of *paying* for it: how can money be collected from the traveller for the service, or from the carrier? Perhaps the system will be offered first by a telephone company, which is in the best position to levy these charges. For more expensive journeys, of course, travel agents, shipping and air lines will plan your itinerary free, because they gain from the sale of the ticket.

From the above examples it can be seen that response

time is one of the most important characteristics of any computer-based system, and in our review of them we shall consider systems in sequence of increasing speed.

Slow-response systems

What kind of questions do *not* require rapid answers? Obviously academic questions—in the sense of pure research —need rapid answers only in so far as the researcher is personally impatient for them. The universe itself has been in existence for some 10 billion years, and a delay of a week in exploring a hypothesis about the circumstances of its origin seems not unreasonable.

The components of a computer-supported research system (it would be insulting to scientists to call it computer-*based*!) are:

(a) The physical entities under study, such as stars, or magnetism,

(b) The objectives of the research team (usually less specific than those of a team working on a business project),

(c) The team's methods and equipment, of which the most important are:

*   (i)   *Equipment* like telescopes, planetary probes, etc. to improve the acuity of their senses,

     (ii)   A symbolic *notation* for describing features of the entities, e.g. distance from earth in *light years*,

    (iii)   *Hypotheses*, expressed as relationships between symbols (e.g. mathematical equations) which enable features of entities to be predicted, given certain other features from observation,

*   (iv)   *Hypothesis-testing techniques*. This could be trivial if the hypothesis was that feature z equals $5x + 6y$, and x, y, and z are given. But if the relationship is very complicated, as in the case of the internal reactions of elements at the core of a star, over a period of millions of years, hypotheses may be impossible to test by hand calculation.

It is in the areas marked with an asterisk that computers are of greatest use. Computers are used for extracting data from signals received by radio or orthodox telescopes, when the signals are mixed with random interference. This technique is employed to separate out the regular pulses emitted by the fainter 'pulsars', by decomposing the apparently random signals into a spectrum of frequencies and finding strongly marked ones. (This same technique is also used to find abnormal behaviour in jet aircraft from their noise.)

But the last area—hypothesis-testing—is even more interesting. When the Cambridge astronomer Professor Fred Hoyle was speculating on how the universe might have come to its present observed state, he hypothesised internal thermo-nuclear and gravitational reactions going on inside stars, and in some cases proposed variations from 'normal' physical laws. The life of a star may be a gradual progression as one particular reaction occurs steadily, but at certain points new reactions can supervene at quite short notice— the most dramatic, of course, being the start of a super-nova. The calculations required to follow the mathematical model of each of a range of stars through their lives are gigantic. This is an ideal application for a computer.

After the computer has run millions of years of star life, in a matter of hours, the population of stars of various kinds can be checked against what we can see: if the real and computer universes are similar, the hypothesis has survived at least one test. It should be pointed out that simulation is not an efficient way of working out problems for which an accurate mathematical formula is known. For example, we might wish to know the volume of a sphere of radius .5 inches. There is a well-known formula: Volume $= \frac{4}{3}\pi r^3$.

This we can evaluate in a few moments for $r = .5''$: volume then $= .52359877$ cubic inches.

But we could find the answer without knowing the value of π or the formula, by simulation. We imagine the sphere inside a cube, one inch each side. We take a point at random inside the cube, and see whether it is also within the sphere. The probability P of its being inside the sphere is obviously equal to the volume of the sphere divided by the volume of the enclosing cube. The cube's volume is easily worked out— 1 inch $\times$ 1 inch $\times$ 1 inch gives us 1 cubic inch. If we now try very many points at random, we expect the proportion of points found inside the sphere to the total of all of them to approach P, and the volume of the sphere may be estimated from P divided by 1, i.e. P itself. We write a little program:

```
10 I = 0                              count of points inside sphere
20 X = .29 : Y = .37 : Z = .53        co-ordinates of first point (random)
30 INPUT N                            ask for number of points to consider
40 FOR L = 1 TO N                     consider them in turn
50 D = SQR ( (X-.5)↑2 + (Y-.5)↑2 + (Z-.5)↑2 )   distance to sphere centre
60 IF D > .5 THEN 80                  go to 80 if point outside the sphere
70 I = I + 1                          point is within the sphere : count it
80 X = RND(X) : Y=RND(Y) : Z=RND(Z)   random choice of next point's
                                      co-ordinates
90 NEXT L                             consider next point, or go to 100 if
                                      all considered
100 PRINT I/N                         print the estimate, I divided by N
110 STOP
```

Fig. 33 *Simulation of $V = \frac{4}{3}\pi r^3$ in BASIC*

When this program is run, one can imagine the points appearing one after another like midges inside the cube, and the computer counting those within the sphere until as many points have been examined as we specified by N. Obviously the more points, the more accurate the result will be, although accuracy is improved more and more slowly:

when		
	10 points were taken, the result was	.7
	100	.39
	1000	.525
	10 000	.5236

The last run took half an hour or so, but was remarkably close to the true figure. For finding the volume of a sphere when the normal formula is available, such a method is absurd, but for peculiar shapes for which no formula is readily available, it can well be used. Note the use of RND to produce random co-ordinates in the range 0 to 1. It may seem strange to introduce deliberate randomness into something as deterministic as a computer, but this technique is common in simulation, e.g. for simulating the random arrival of customers at a GPO counter. More is said about this kind of simulation later in this chapter.

One last point on the program. It was written in BASIC, a simple but powerful language. Line 50 uses Pythagoras to find the distance from the point to the sphere centre: the ↑ sign denotes 'raised to the power of', and SQR denotes 'square root'. Note that the program could be made more efficient by eliminating the square root, and testing in line 60 against the *square* of the sphere's radius, i.e. .25″.

We may also reflect on the price of accuracy: our aim should be to provide that degree of accuracy which minimises the *total* cost, of both the inaccuracy itself, and the cost of computation.

Running slow-response programs as 'background' jobs

Very large, long scientific computer jobs are given a low priority in a general-purpose computer installation—perhaps run at night, or over a weekend. They tend to make great demands on the central processor's arithmetic circuitry, working on figures in its own memory, and less demands on the peripherals—file storage units, card readers, line printers, etc. The usage pattern is rather different from most business jobs like the Sales Accounting system described in the last chapter. This suggests an alternative to segregating big scientific jobs to nights and weekends.

Suppose we are running our Sales Accounting program

and the COBOL program has just reached the instruction:

READ TRANS-FILE

The Operating System in most systems will have anticipated this instruction and already called for 80 characters from the card reader, and tries to have this information waiting ready in part of the central processor's memory known as a 'buffer' so that the READ *effectively* transfers the information from the buffer to FORM-RECORD, and tells the card reader to re-fill the buffer with the *next* card. Hence there is *at best* a delay of only a few microseconds after READ, not the milliseconds involved in the mechanical operation of the card reader. However, it may well happen that the card reader is reading at its maximum speed during the sales accounting run, and all the other parts of the computer—particularly the central processor—are under-loaded, even if the buffer technique is used. Even if the computer is reading not actual cards but 'card images' from magnetic tape or disc (placed there by a previous off-lining/spooling operation), the speed of the tape or disc unit is still too slow to avoid wasted central processor power. It is a pity to have this spare power lying idle, when it could be used on a job like Hoyle's star model. Ideally we should like these two complementary programs to be run together—'multi-programmed'.

It will be seen that we can speak loosely of a multi-programming computer 'doing two jobs at once' but actually the computer is switching rapidly between jobs, according to the *part* of the computer which is under-employed at any one time. Furthermore there would be no point in loading a computer with jobs which make heavy demands on the same part of it.

At first sight it may seem we have to write one big program using the EVENT technique discussed in the previous chapter, and including both SALE01 and the star model. In fact, the operating system is capable of loading several

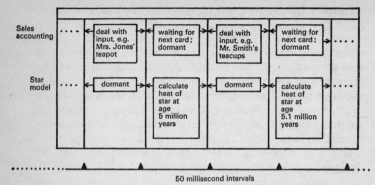

Fig. 34 *Activity of central processor during multi-programming*

programs into the central processor's memory at a time. Whenever the high priority program (SALE01) is held up waiting for the card reader (or a disc or tape unit, or the printer), the operating system passes control to the low priority program (the star model). This then calculates temperatures and pressures until the circuitry controlling the transfer of information from one of the peripherals sends a signal which breaks the regular sequence of instructions in the star model program, and makes the central processor start executing some instructions in the operating system. These instructions decide whether SALE01 can proceed, and if so, record where the star model program had got to (so it can resume in the right place). This technique is known as *multi-programming*, using *interrupts*. When the central processor's memory is divided into areas semi-permanently for jobs of various sizes, like the walls in a western house, the operating system is said to have *fixed partitions*: if it can adjust the number and the positions of the boundaries (like screens in a Japanese house) according to the mixture of jobs and their sizes, it is said to be *multi-programming with a variable number of tasks*.

Of course it can be very irritating to have your program

assigned a low priority and given only the scraps of computer processing which fall from the table of the high priority jobs. Accordingly it is possible for the operating system to be interrupted by a sort of electronic stopwatch at regular intervals (say two seconds), at which time it reallocates control to another program, and may even temporarily move out the old program and its half-finished results in memory, into a disc unit, in order to make room for the new one. Such a scheme is used in 'timesharing' systems, to be discussed later.

Simulation

But we have digressed into the technicalities of running the slow-response star model as economically as possible. What would such a program look like? Firstly, it is likely to be written in the scientific languages FORTRAN or ALGOL, or possibly PL/1.

It will represent some model we have of the star's behaviour: it *simulates* the star's life, a second of computer time being equivalent to thousands of years of star time. For example we may consider the star to be a perfect sphere of radius r, and composed of a homogeneous material.

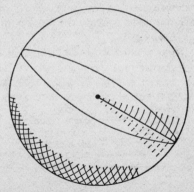

Fig. 35 *Idealised star model divided into 15 concentric shells*

We may take say 15 points along *r* and assume that inside the intervals between them, temperature and pressure are constant, and that all radii are the same. Our star is now conceptually an onion.

Suppose we have a hunch that the temperatures and pressures have particular values at star age one million years, and we also have a theory based on chemical and nuclear reactions that, if a shell of the assumed homogeneous material is at pressure *P* and temperature *T*, after a thousand years *P* and *T* change to *P'* and *T'*. But in addition, the pressure and temperature of its neighbouring shells on either side will change *P'* and *T'* further, to *P''* and *T''*. Then another thousand years pass, and so on. Perhaps our theory about how *P'* and *T'* depend on earlier *P* and *T* includes a proviso that if *P* or *T* exceed a given value, different laws apply. It is not obvious whether our theory will result in the star collapsing, or blowing up, or if so, when.

(As a matter of fact the idealised star model above is not Hoyle's, and is actually a very poor model, because of the convection currents which may stir up the layers continuously. It corresponds to an incorrect hypothesis and if the results of the simulation do, unfortunately, fit what is actually observed, we hope the experimenter takes the cautious view mentioned earlier, that 'the hypothesis has survived at least one test' and go on to design other tests before shouting '*Eureka!*'.)

Overall, our program might look like that of Fig. 36:

```
COMMON P (15), T (15), AGE
CALL STARSTART          ┌─ cycle executed 1000 times,
DO 1 I = 1, 1000 ───────┤  each cycle of 10 000 000 years
CALL PRINTSTAR          └─
DO 2 J = 1, 10000 ──────┐  cycle executed
AGE = AGE + 1000        │  10 000 times,
CALL NEWSTAR            │  each cycle of
2   CONTINUE◄───────────┘  1000 years
1   CONTINUE◄
STOP
```

Fig. 36 *Skeleton of star model program: Fortran.*

Note that names like STARSTART may have to be abbreviated in practice.

This program is written in FORTRAN and begins with a call on a procedure to set the starting conditions for the star—our guesses at its temperatures and pressures in its youth. We then repeat the steps down to 1 a thousand times, which include a call on a procedure to print the nature of the star at this point in its career. Obviously the first occasion will just echo the starting conditions.

The steps include an interior cycle of three steps repeated 10 000 times in which the next state of the star is calculated by formulae in 'NEWSTAR' as a function of its previous state, over a period of a thousand years.

Note that more than one set of formulae (LORULES and HIRULES) may be applied, depending on the temperature and pressure: e.g.

```
      SUBROUTINE NEWSTAR
      COMMON P (15), T (15), AGE
      DO 3 N = 1, 15
      IF ((P(N).GT.18900).AND.(T(N).GT.6000)) GOTO 4
      CALL LORULES
      GOTO 3
    4 CALL HIRULES
    3 CONTINUE
      DO 5 N = 1, 10
      CALL BALANCE
    5 CONTINUE
      RETURN
      END
```

Fig. 37 *Calculating the new state of the star: Fortran*

So 1000 'snapshots' are printed by PRINTSTAR at intervals of 10 000 000 years. Now the procedure NEWSTAR itself cycles through the assumed 15 intervals to calculate their temperatures and pressures, and then perform further balancing, say 10 times, to gain an equilibrium of temperature and pressure along the radius. Balancing itself will involve scanning the 15 intervals. This means that the innermost operation, calculating the temperature and pressure of a particular interval along the radius, may be repeated

$$(15 + (10 \times 15)) \times 10\,000 \times 1000$$
$$= 1\,650\,000\,000 \text{ times}$$

The calculations may involve several high precision multiplications and divisions taking say 100 microseconds to compute. Hence the total time for the job will be roughly

$$\frac{100}{1\,000\,000} \text{ secs} \times 1\,650\,000\,000 \text{ or two days non-stop.}$$

This kind of operation is termed *number-crunching*!

By various refinements we could perhaps speed it up—terminating the program if the star is moribund, e.g.

IF (P(1).LT.0.0001) STOP

i.e. if pressure at the centre of the star is Less Than some small value we can assume everything interesting has already happened.

A very similar problem is that of calculating temperature, pressure, humidity, and movement in cells of atmosphere, for *weather forecasting*. The 'starting values' are provided by observations from meteorological stations and balloons, and the state of each cell repeatedly recalculated until its age corresponds with the mid-point of the next forecast period. Then the practical effects of the cells' states—sunshine or shower—are calculated and advised to the public.

Obviously a two-day delay would make the forecasts useless. But fortunately the advantages of weather forecasting make it economic to buy large computers devoted to this task, and at Bracknell the Meteorological Office has one of the largest machines, an IBM/360 model 195.

Of course we could use cheaper, slower computers for this kind of task if we reduced the number of computation cycles performed, by increasing the time represented by one cycle, from 1000 years to 10 000 years (or from five minutes to an hour, for weather forecasts). Similarly the number of intervals along the radius could be cut, or the size of atmosphere cells increased. But we then run the risk of oversimplifying our model—rather as if Dunlop and Good-year designed wheels as polygons, but to save effort, reduced the number of sides from 4000 to four—which would *not* be an accurate approximation. The weather forecasting system is therefore designed to provide a reasonable degree of precision, and response to the observational data measured in hours, and at this performance level gives the best value for money. British Airways (Overseas Division), can, for example, clip several minutes flying time off North Atlantic flights by using the BABS computer to work out the path which avoids headwinds and seeks tailwinds, using information transmitted from Bracknell. An interesting technique is employed in this computer system: because the calculations are extensive, it is not easy to make the response time very rapid at the times of day when flight planners, at London, New York and elsewhere, want the computer results for particular flights: this is because the computer complex will be busy with reservations and departure processing. Accordingly flight plans are calculated in the night for a whole range of possible flights and stored ready for use. Only some of these may be used in practice, but it is cheaper to precalculate a few extra unnecessary plans at off-peak time, than to calculate just the necessary ones at peak times.

Two further observations can be made about the star model and weather forecasting. Firstly, in the star model we are trying to find out if the *formulae* correctly represent the inside of a star: they may be right if, for a whole range of initial conditions, the stars we get out of the model seem like the stars we can observe. But in weather forecasting we are fairly confident about our formulae and the outcome is a prediction. The two systems represent aspects of *simulation* —firstly model building and validation by observation, then after validation, extrapolating into the future to predict (whether it will rain tomorrow, or whether our sun will shrink or explode). In a sense all computer programs are simulations, but the term is used particularly of those which represent the passing of real-world time by an internal cycle.

Secondly both models assume a fixed 'clockwork' nature and ignore possible random events such as collisions with comets. Computer simulations can in fact take these into account if necessary. Suppose a comet may collide with a star with a probability of .001 in any period of 1000 years. One cannot realistically build into the calculations, repeated at 1000 year intervals, a mini-comet of .001 size colliding— nor make a full-size one collide regularly every

$$\frac{1000}{.001} = 1\ 000\ 000 \text{ years}$$

which would not model the effects of several comets striking in relatively quick succession, which must sometimes happen. What we can do is program the computer to 'toss a coin' which determines whether a random event has happened or not. Many operating systems will supply a program with an effectively random number on demand, for example one lying between 0 and 1, e.g. 0.37789138. The programmer can write IF(RANDNO.GT. 0.999) CALL COMET and CALL COMET will be reached when RANDNO takes values .9991, .9997, etc., which it will do on .001 occasions.

Such simulations are termed 'probabilistic' and are used for modelling queues of people in Post Offices (where the arrival of a new customer at a given instant of time is determined by the random number), or ships at a tanker terminal, cars at a roundabout, and even the loading on a computer itself as in the sort of case discussed in the last chapter, where ten typewriters are connected, and occasionally all typists will press a key in the same tenth of a second: can the program cope? Such probabilistic simulations are liable to take even longer to give useful results because we have to wait until a sufficient number of random occurrences have been dealt with for the behaviour of the modelled real-life process to become stable and statistically reliable. This is termed the 'settling' time.

One of the most famous computer simulation experiments is in the field of world economics. In *World Dynamics* by Jay W. Forrester, a model is set up of the major factors governing human economic life:

(a) Population
(b) Natural Resources available
(c) Level of Capital Investment
(d) Pollution

all of which interact over time to produce a 'quality of life' factor. The interactions were defined as formulae (e.g. pollution is a function of the rate of natural resource depletion in the preceding years) and simulations were run to model various scenarios such as the acceptance of birth control, etc. All the results were gloomy in the extreme, and some critics have pointed out that the formulae are partly conjectural, and in some cases a slightly more optimistic version of them will change the overall predictions markedly. This leads us to the general observation that the *sensitivity* of a model to various assumptions must be investigated before we can be confident that the model is a good predictor. (In the star case, if our own sun was only 25% more massive, it would already have burned out, so equations in a star model which involve mass must be fairly precise.)

Corporate Planning

Much economic modelling is done for very practical reasons by companies interested in the next ten years ahead, not the next 100. A sophisticated business typically plans as follows (see Fig. 38).

The really crucial figures, which will determine survival and growth, are the cash, profit, and asset figures at the end of the current year. These figures must look right to shareholders and other sources of finance; must be realizable, and, in the event, realized. This last must be achieved by the efforts of production, sales, and distribution.

Short term expedients to keep on annual targets	ad hoc
Plan next year ahead month by month to achieve final targets	annually or ad hoc if a major upset occurs
Plan next two years in quarters	annually
Plan next five years in whole years	annually
Plan next 10 years in whole years	annually

Fig. 38 *Business planning horizons*

But to ensure the figures look right and are realizeable, the sophisticated company plans them, long in advance, in broad outline, after making best assumptions about markets, technology, and competition. Ten years ago the current targets were part of a ten year plan in which, perhaps, provision was made for 'a new product' or 'a new factory' and at that stage nobody had decided exactly what the new product would be, except perhaps in general terms such as 'diversification into consumer market'. Five years ago this year's plan became firmer and two years ago cash flows would be calculated fairly accurately. One year ago the agreement of the managers was obtained to their accepting this year's plan as a commitment. (This is in strong contrast to the small entrepreneurial venture which conceives an idea for a new service or product in considerable detail, then tries to market it, and only at the end looks at the long-term financial picture.)

The large company's financial planners prepare very many ten, five, and two-year plans every year—on each occasion they *simulate* a different set of assumptions, and stop only when they have a plan which is consistent with best assumptions, gives the best long-term outcome in the light of corporate objectives, and is consistent with the company's present position.

Each of the 'trial' plans has formulae in it like those in the star model. Investment in a given period depends on:

Cash resources
Ability to raise finance
Sales of assets

Cash resources depend on

Profit in last period and brought forward
Distributions to shareholders
Tax

and these relationships can be as complicated to define as any scientific reaction, as was pointed out by Mr. Paul Chambers, former Chairman of ICI. Moreover the future impact of items like 'tax' may have to be guessed from government White Papers and party manifestos.

A range of ready-made programs or *packages* (in the jargon) are available from computer manufacturers and consultants. (Packages tend to be produced for computer systems which are essentially similar whatever organisation is involved: 'payroll' is a good example.) For example:

PROMISE (IBM)
PROSPER (International Computers Ltd.)
FORESIGHT (Timesharing Ltd.)

Large companies sometimes produce their own, like BP's 'FIRM' (Financially Integrated Refining and Marketing).

More general-purpose simulation packages, suitable for modelling docks and GPO counters, include:

GPSS (General Purpose Simulation System)
SIMSCRIPT
CSL (Control and Simulation Language)
SIMULA
Continuous System Modelling Program

Interactive Corporate Planning

We have called long-range planning systems 'slow-response', but in some cases they are designed, not to run through voluminous calculations representing years of corporate activity possibility after possibility, but to work with a human planner who directs the simulation into the most promising areas.

He will sit at a computer terminal (see last chapter) and set up some assumptions, e.g.

(a) TAX rate in 1980 estimate: 50% of PROFIT except on profit from factories in development areas—10%
(b) NEW FACTORY in 1979: LOCATION . . .
(c) NEW PRODUCT LAUNCH 1981: REVENUE . . .

The computer will recalculate its plan and give estimates on profit, cash flow, etc. year by year: the planner studies these and perhaps alters some assumptions (e.g. postpone PRODUCT LAUNCH) and runs again. Such a partnership is very productive, and uses the ability of the computer to calculate consequences quickly and accurately, and of the human being, to apply 'hunches' to achieve a good solution instead of going blindly through millions of combinations.

In such a system *either* the human partner waits a day or so for the results of his proposals, and in the meantime does something else, *or* he can sit at a terminal and get the results back in seconds. In the latter case he has the advantage of maintaining a flow of ideas without interruption, and can achieve more in less elapsed time: very convenient when the Board of Directors is meeting tomorrow to discuss policy. It should, however, be pointed out that such *on-line interactive* systems can be wasteful, in that the human partner becomes tired and proposes unproductive hunches. (One use of interactive systems is in programming itself. Programmers can however waste a great deal of time trying various corrections to a program that does not work, instead of leaving the terminal, having a coffee, and really thinking.)

So such *on-line interactive* systems, which do the same job as the slow-response simulation programs, really need quite rapid responses for the human partner to keep his flow of concentration. To achieve this, the technique of time-sharing is employed. The big simulation program is brought into the central processor's memory by the operating system from its normal residence on a disc unit, whenever the terminal operator keys in some new direction, and works away on it until perhaps suspended for a while by a higher priority job, or because it is the turn of another terminal to have a *share* of the computer's *time*, in which case it is 'rolled out' on to the disc for a second or two, then 'rolled in' again.

We should mention three other important computer-based systems used, like simulation over time, for modelling situations and suggesting what should be done to achieve the best outcome:

Project Evaluation Review Technique (PERT), based on Critical Path Analysis (CPA), is used to analyse complicated project plans, in which various activities cannot start until others have been completed, as in the building of nuclear-powered submarines (where the idea originated). If it is reported that delivery of a particular component is running late, the system can work out whether this will affect the completion of the overall project, or, if not, how much 'slack' there is before it *will* start to affect it. One can visualise a project as a network of activities (see Fig. 39).

The lines represent *activities* and the small circles, *events* marking the completion of an activity. The dotted line is a 'dummy activity' showing that installing the engine room cannot start until the keel is laid, as well as the reactor procured. The figures in brackets indicate 'expected elapsed time', in weeks or months. Obviously the heavy line is

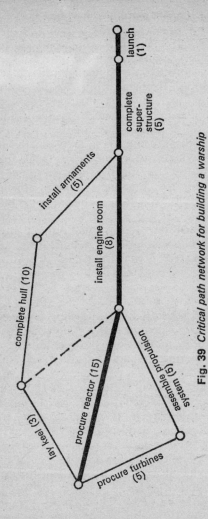

Fig. 39 *Critical path network for building a warship*

launch
(1)

complete
super-
structure
(5)

install armaments
(5)

install engine room
(8)

complete hull (10)

procure reactor (15)

assemble propulsion
system (5)

lay keel (3)

procure turbines
(5)

critical, and the launch will not be affected by a slippage on laying the keel until this exceeds five time-units. If there is a problem on the *critical* activities, management should rob resources from the non-critical.

The example is trivially simple, but projects involving thousands of activities are common, and a computer system is ideal for analysing them before the projects start, to help in planning and estimating, and after they have started, to record progress and point out situations where a delay has become critical.

Sometimes Critical Path Analysis can prevent unnecessary anxiety. There is an anecdote about the launch of a new engine in the Ford Motor Company: during a progress meeting, one manager reported a delay on the supply of a big machine tool. This caused considerable alarm and it was some time before it was realised that this particular machine tool did not need to be available until later anyway.

Computer projects themselves are suitable subjects for Critical Path Analysis. 'Packages' are available from computer manufacturers and consultants.

Mathematical programming, in particular linear programming, is the second technique which tends to be grouped with simulations and Critical Path Analysis; 'programming' is not a reference to computer programming at all but to a mathematical approach. It is a scientific way of finding the right *combination* of resources, whether machines, or materials, or people, to apply in order to get the optimum result. For example animal feedstuffs must contain certain levels of vitamins, calories, protein etc., and are mixtures of ingredients each contributing to the requirements. If the costs of the ingredients change, it may be worthwhile varying the mixture. To take a simplified example, the contributions and prices of three ingredients might be:

Ingredient	X	Y	Z	
Cost	5	8	4	pence/lb
Vitamin A	10	10	5	units per lb
Protein	50	48	55	
Iron	5	10	0	

Fig. 40 *Foodstuff costs and requirements*

What mixture is cheapest if the minimum requirements are:

Vitamin A	8	Units
Protein	50	per
Iron	6	lb

Fig. 41 *Minimum nutritional content*

We can write equations as follows: let the proportion of ingredients X, Y, Z be

$$X\%$$
$$Y\%$$
$$100\% - X\% - Y\%$$

respectively. Then the total cost of a pound of mixture will be:

$(X\% \times 5) + (Y\% \times 8) + ((100 - X - Y)\% \times 4)$ pence.

But we are subject to the limits given above, so

$(X\% \times 10) + (Y\% \times 10) + ((100 - X - Y)\% \times 5) \geqslant 8$
$(X\% \times 50) + (Y\% \times 48) + ((100 - X - Y)\% \times 55) \geqslant 50$
and
$(X\% \times 5) + (Y\% \times 10) \geqslant 6$

(The sign '$\geqslant$' means 'equal to or greater than')

The answer to the problem is in fact 54% of ingredient X, 33% of Y, and 13% of Z (to the nearest 1%):

Ingredient %	X 54	Y 33	Z 13	Totals	
Cost	2·70	2·64	0·52	5·86	pence/lb
Vitamin A	5·40	3·30	0·65	9·35	units per lb
Protein	27·00	15·85	7·15	50·00	
Iron	2·70	3·30	00·00	6·00	

Fig. 42 *Least cost food mixture*

It will be seen that this meets the Protein and Iron requirements and provides extra vitamin A. However, if we try to
economise on vitamin A by adding more Z, we shall fail to
provide enough iron.

Most real problems of course have many more ingredients
than three, and the solution may be found most easily by a
computer-based linear programming formulation. The
animal feedstuffs problem is a real one, and Barker and Lee
Smith, a producer of feedstuffs, use a Texas Instruments
980A computer for linear programming in this area.

The response time of such a system is governed by the
volatility of ingredient prices and the ability of the firm to
vary purchases and recipes quickly on the one hand, and the
cost of frequent recalculations on the other. The author
used this technique for a long term survey of resources—
knitting capacity, dye house throughput, etc.—needed by
Pasolds Ltd., the manufacturer of children's Ladybird
clothes, to produce a range of garments at maximum profit.
The exercise also identifies which resources are *critical*, e.g.
we note that in the foodstuff example, we have to use the
expensive ingredient Y solely because we cannot provide the
iron content otherwise. This may prompt a search for a
cheaper source of iron.

Linear programming has been extensively employed in the
oil industry to determine the best mixture of products to

refine from crude oil, and in every field where one is trying to *maximise* a value like profit, or *minimise* cost, or, more generally, *optimise* some value which is a function of our choice of resources to use. In addition there are usually *constraints* on what we can do (e.g. although the most profitable product may be aviation gasoline, it is impossible to make this alone).

Other mathematical programming techniques cover situations where relationships are not simple, linear ones: e.g. quadratic programming and dynamic programming. This last is nothing to do with an energetic computer professional, except in so far as the technique is commonly applied on a computer. Dynamic programming often involves the time element again, like simulation: applications include scheduling vehicles by the shortest route (the North Atlantic flight planning system mentioned earlier uses the technique), and purchasing or selling high value commodities like gold and tungsten when prices are liable to fluctuate.

Statistical analysis. The techniques described above give managers an insight into some situations where there are factors which they can manipulate, and suggest how they should be manipulated to give best results.

Statistical analysis on the other hand might be said to give insight into situations outside, or partly outside, our control, and to uncover relationships between the factors. For example, statistical analysis may reveal that antisocial children have on average a significantly higher level of lead in their bodies than children as a whole. When we have ruled out other possible explanations of this relationship (such as that antisocial children tend to bite objects coated in paint containing lead, or that living near a main road causes *both* antisocial tendencies *and* exposure to lead from exhaust emissions), we may be confident we should remove children from exposure to lead and so make them less antisocial.

In marketing, computers are used by A. C. Nielsen and

Co. near Oxford for extracting such relationships to ensure that when their clients spend money on promoting a new product or service, it is directed at those people most likely to buy it. Information is obtained about the market, for example, by interviewing members of the public and noting their answers to carefully phrased questions on a form. These forms have to be converted—as described in Chapter 2—into a form acceptable to the computer, either by operators transcribing the symbols into punched cards or tape, or by running the forms through a document reader capable of detecting well-written digits or simply pencil strokes such as the IBM 3881 Optical Mark Reader:

			Box
DO YOU NOW OWN ONE OR MORE DOGS?	[ ]	Yes	A
Mark one only:	[ ]	No	B
IF SO, HOW OLD IS IT (OR HOW OLD IS THE OLDEST)?	[ ]	under 1 yr.	C
	[ ]	1 or over, but under 3	D
(Mark none if answer to previous question was 'no', otherwise mark one of three)	[ ]	3 or over	E

Fig. 43 *Small part of computer-readable questionnaire*

The program will check the form for validity, e.g. if 'A' means 'box A has a mark in it', we can write (in FORTRAN):

```
IF (A.EQ.B) CALL BADAB
IF (A.AND..NOT.(C.OR.D.OR.E)) CALL NOAGE
IF ((C.AND.D).OR.(C.AND.E).OR.(D.AND.E)) CALL BADCDE
```
Fig. 44 *Checking validity of input: FORTRAN*

(You may note that A.EQ.B is a convenient way of testing for the mistakes of marking both or neither, and that the last test will register an error if all three are marked.)

After *validation* to remove incorrect forms, the program will go on to count occurrences of different respondents and to print a final result, e.g.

```
TOTAL RESPONDENTS:          1280
REJECTED FORMS                36
ANALYSED                    1244
   DOG OWNERS                709
     .
     .
     .

DOG OWNERS WITH ONE OR MORE
DOGS ALL UNDER 3 YEARS OLD   206 = 29%
     .
     .
     .
```

Fig. 45 *Statistical analysis—marketing*

This information might help a marketing manager in lpanning an approach to a particular market, for example, to decide whether advertising might be directed at owners of puppies, with good results.

Instead of writing a special program for each analysis we do, we can often make use of a general purpose statistical analysis *package* program, examples of which are:

XTAB   Survey analysis
GENSTAT   Statistical analysis generally
ASCOP   Editing and analysis

The computer may have attached to it a *graph plotter* as a peripheral device which has a pen under program control, which can be made to draw pie charts, histograms, etc. (see also Fig. 46).

Such graph plotters can of course draw other shapes as well, like engineering layouts and 'computer art' pictures. It is also possible to use the ordinary computer printer to draw shapes from a mosaic of letters, just as a typewriter can produce a graph or even an approximation of the Mona Lisa.

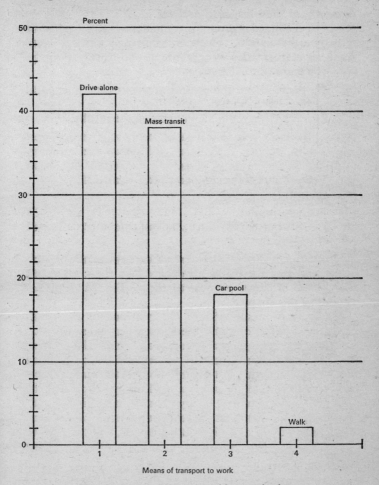

Fig. 46 *Histogram produced by graph plotter*
(courtesy WANG)

Summary of 'slow-response' systems

We have examined a group of computer systems—scientific research, simulation, business planning, Critical Path Analysis, mathematical programming, and statistical analysis—which are characterised by:

(a) Big demands on the central processor's mathematical powers and memory,

(b) Relative lack of urgency in getting the results.

Nevertheless, we note that if rapid response is needed after all, as with weather forecasting and interactive company planning, there are ways of getting the results out faster than just waiting for the computer's free week-end:

(a) Multiprogramming,

(b) Timesharing,

(c) and, of course, providing a big fast computer, dedicated to the job in hand.

To quote the old Spanish proverb: 'God says, take what you want: and pay for it.' It all depends on the cost/benefit trade-off of different response times; see Fig. 32 at the beginning of this chapter.

The systems described are the province of the 'philosophers' among computer users: the operational research practitioners, management scientists and statisticians. These men or women are generally mathematicians by training and will be found (in most organisations) in the Management Services function along with the work study people and the computer programmers, analysts, and operations staff. However, it is hoped that the reader now has an impression of the scope of the techniques they deploy, and can turn to these experts if he feels there is an opportunity for their services.

4

Medium-response Computer-based Systems

The great majority of computers spend most of their time working to a regular time-table, such as, for example, Fig. 47.

It is a tricky task to schedule the work to meet the requirements of the organisation (we *must* have the pay ready to distribute on Friday) while placing an even load on the computer. Usually this means loading it with a regular *weekly* schedule, with variations to allow for extra work at month ends (when SALE01 produces invoices and statements) and year ends (tax returns for employees, stock taking, etc.).

The slow-response, thoughtful jobs described in the preceding chapter are allocated to Wednesday A and Sunday A and B, and we will have no hesitation in cancelling them despite the protests of the management scientists, if we need the time for invoicing or payroll. The same goes for program testing.

As we saw in the last chapter, modern computers often 'multi-program' their jobs so that the above timetable may refer not to the whole computer but to the loading on one of its *partitions*, and there may be another timetable for other partitions just as if the computer was, schizophrenically, several independent computers. On a yet more advanced computer with variable partitions, we can load it up with jobs, each with a date/time when it must be finished, and let the operating system decide how to run them (it may well

Shift	Mon	Tues	Wed	Thurs	Fri	Sat	Sun
A	PRODUC-TION CONTROL	PRODUC-TION AND STOCK CONTROL	MANAGE-MENT SCIENCE	MAINTEN-ANCE	ORDER PROCES-SING		RESEARCH
B	STOCK CONTROL	PURCHASE LEDGER	SOFTWARE	PROGRAM TEST	SALE01		RESEARCH
C	PROGRAM TEST	PROGRAM TEST	PROGRAM TEST	PAYROLL	SALE01*		PROGRAM TEST*

* Last Friday in month only. Otherwise Friday shift C is program test and Sunday shift is cancelled

Fig. 47 *Computer time-table example*

use a scheduling system like Critical Path Analysis for its own operations). Nevertheless, however sophisticated the method of achieving it, we must have a target timetable as illustrated in Fig. 47, for the results to emerge (usually as printed paper) and distributed to the human part of the system concerned. We can now see how the computer supplies the computer element to several different computer-based systems:

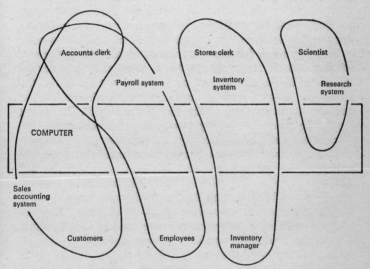

Fig. 48 *One computer can support several computer-based systems, simultaneously or in alternation*

Sales accounting

Let us look at some of the bread and butter jobs which have to be done regularly, typically once a week. In fact our first example, SALE01, is a suitable one to begin with.

Why was a week chosen for the basic response time of this system?

Firstly the accounts section may well be organised to meet a weekly cycle. If other jobs like payroll are scheduled to a weekly timetable, the clerks have a regular, balanced work pattern.

Secondly, a more frequent run, e.g. daily would involve increasing the overheads in running the job on the computer: putting special stationery in the computer printer, and mounting tapes or discs containing the customer and product files, for example. We could also find ourselves sending five letters to customers instead of one, each week.

Thirdly, a *less* frequent run would mean that at the end of the month there would be a significant number of deliveries in the pipeline which were not yet known to the computer system, and so could not be included on the invoices to be sent out at the end of the month. The result would be a delay in getting money in for goods which had been sold, and consequentially, an increase in bank overdraft and interest charges. It may be objected that we could run SALE01 on the last Friday of the month *only*, and still be able to invoice all deliveries: but unfortunately a proportion of the information on the forms will have errors on it—incorrect customer or product codes—which the computer program will reject, and must be corrected and re-submitted. It is better to do this regularly through the month so as to have the maximum amount of correct deliveries to invoice at the end. From the cash collection aspect, it is advantageous to allocate *payments* to customers' accounts frequently, so that we know quickly if a payment does not seem to match a customer's indebtedness. In particular, if he has not paid by the required date, we do not want to wait a whole month before sending him a reminder or even stopping further supplies.

Conversely if a customer is 'on stop' for non-payment, we want to resume trading with him promptly after he has paid up. Again, when we receive cash payments, we want to allocate them to customers' accounts quickly and get the money into the bank.

The accountants are also keen to record the transfer of goods from stock, where they are valued at *production cost*, to the sales ledger (i.e. customer file) where they are valued at *sales price*. This transfer means that the company accounts show more profit. The accountants are particularly keen to have this done at the end of the financial year, and it is at this time that a decent response time in sales accounting helps them. One may think this is just 'window-dressing', but the company accounts, when published, must show the profitability of the company in the best light to attract and maintain investment.

Of course, the choice of a weekly cycle may be wrong for a different company with different accounting schedules, customers, and products, but the same general considerations will determine what cycle is chosen. A cost–benefit chart like Fig. 32 can be drawn, and the optimum cycle chosen.

Sales invoicing is one of the commonest computer applications. It is concerned with the collection of cash—the life-blood of an organisation—and with the delicate balance between losing money and irritating customers with premature or incorrect invoices. Because each company's products and market are unique, sales invoicing is usually specially designed, although some sales invoicing 'packages' are offered, e.g. CMG offer a package to run on the Burroughs 2500 computer. Printing the invoice is only part of the system: at least as important is keeping track of the customer's indebtedness. Traditionally this is done by entries—credits for payments and allowances, and debits for invoiced deliveries—in a sales ledger by customer. In a computer system the sales ledger is often expanded into a customer file which includes much more information of value not just to the accountant, but to sales, distribution and marketing:

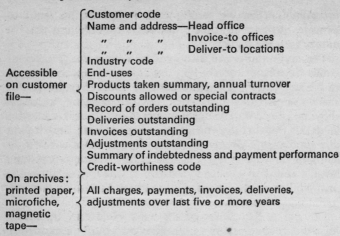

Accessible on customer file—
{
Customer code
Name and address—Head office
    "   "   "   Invoice-to offices
    "   "   "   Deliver-to locations
Industry code
End-uses
Products taken summary, annual turnover
Discounts allowed or special contracts
Record of orders outstanding
Deliveries outstanding
Invoices outstanding
Adjustments outstanding
Summary of indebtedness and payment performance
Credit-worthiness code
}

On archives: printed paper, microfiche, magnetic tape—
{
All charges, payments, invoices, deliveries, adjustments over last five or more years
}

Fig. 49 *Contents of a Customer file*

It is also necessary to have available a *product* file containing:

> Product code
> Description
> Price (or price table by quantity etc.)
> VAT rates

and for purposes of stock control (to be discussed)

> Quantity available for sale
> Quantity allocated and to whom
> Replenishments expected to be supplied from factory, by dates
> Demand patterns
> } for each stock-holding warehouse

Fig. 50 *Contents of a Product file*

In the little SALE01 system, we dealt only with the task of maintaining the Product and Customer files and printing monthly invoices and statements. Invoicing involves taking each product delivered, and multiplying quantity by price, totalling the results, and adding taxes, delivery charges, etc., printing the invoice, and recording the amount either by adding it to the balance outstanding, or by storing the invoice information separately.

We noted that SALE01 would also action payments, but did not specify how this would be done. There are two methods—either the amount of the payment is simply deducted from the balance outstanding ('balance forward method'), cr the payment is matched with the original invoice which triggered it ('open item method'). The difficulty of the first method is that if the balance outstanding stands at a figure, say of £350, it is difficult to tell which invoice or invoices have not been paid, or only partially paid. If the accounts department has an argument with the customer, it has little help from the computer. In the second method, each payment 'crosses off' the corresponding invoice or invoices leaving the unpaid ones clear. However, this does imply that the customer will tell us which invoices his cheque covers, by returning a payment slip with it. This slip will show the original invoice number, and provided the amount on the cheque agrees or is within a few pence—to be 'written off' at the discretion of the cash clerk—the slip will be passed for transcription to computer readable form. For very large systems like electricity billing, the slip may have the invoice number in a form which can be read by a document reader, so avoiding the need for *human* data transcription to cards or tape.

You can see from this system that as a customer you can cause problems by failing to return the payment slip (in which case the cash clerk must obtain a list of invoices to you outstanding and guess which one(s) you are paying), or by paying too much: the system will have to hold the excess payment to set off against future invoices, or send you a credit note for the overpayment. If you pay too little your cheque may be returned, or the invoice cleared but a new invoice, or *debit* note sent to you for the balance. The

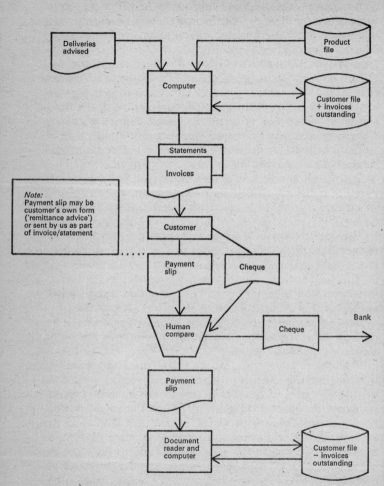

Fig. 51 *'Open item' invoicing and cash collection*

difficulties of the cash posting clerk in an 'open item' system, when deciding whether to accept a cheque and which invoice(s) it relates to, can be handled in three ways. The computer can be programmed to try itself to match the payment. If, for example, there are four invoices outstanding (1, 2, 3 and 4) with values £T(1), £T(2), £T(3) and £T(4), the computer could compare each combination in turn with the cash £C, find the closest match, and assume these were the invoices involved, provided the lowest difference was less than some limit like £10 (see Fig. 52).

This is quick for four invoices, but the computer time doubles for every additional outstanding invoice!

Secondly, the computer can print out, during each weekly run, a complete statement on every customer likely to send in cash, and this paper can be filed by the clerks for reference. This makes for a sea of paper. It is possible, however, to arrange for the computer to produce not paper, but microfilm, or small microfilm cards called microfiches, which the clerks can view through magnifying readers. This is faster and cheaper.

Microfilm and microfiche equipment are marketed by Bell and Howell, 3M, Kodak, and NCR.

The first 'frame' of such a fiche can be an index which tells the inquirer on which frame, i.e. page, the information he seeks is to be found.

The files and systems we have set up for the benefits of the accountants will also be useful for the marketing manager, who will be able to use the information about customers for his market planning exercises—a typical 'slow response' computer job as described in Chapter 3. And the arrangement by which the customer file—or selected parts of it—can be examined at any time, may be exploited to help in the *order-taking* process by providing positive checks on addresses and credit-worthiness, if necessary while the customer is on the telephone.

It is interesting to note, that the very fact that the sales

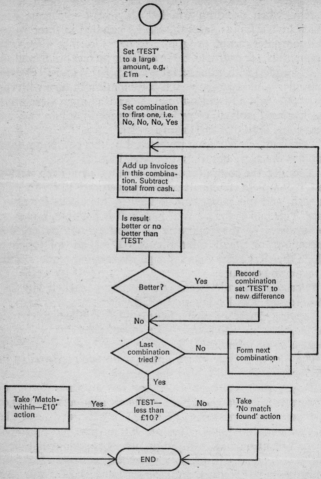

Fig. 52 *Logic block diagram for matching invoices and cash*

Fig. 53 *The girl is holding a 6" × 4" microfiche containing 270 pages of information, produced from computer magnetic tape by the NCR equipment shown.*

accounting system can offer information to other people in the organisation besides the accountants, may make life more difficult for the analyst. He will have to ensure that all those managers with a valid interest in the contribution of the computer to their systems, are invited to join the committee which sponsors and steers the design of the files, decisions and response time, and so on. In general it is easiest if there is one, dominant user of the system, who incurs most of the costs and reaps most of the benefits, but who will magnanimously make available the 'by-products' to other interested parties, who do not then pay much (or have much say in the design).

But if the system must satisfy *several* departments' needs so as to be economically justifiable, there is a serious risk of politics causing hold-ups and argument, unless their common boss intervenes. As a rule of thumb, the analyst should not try, or be used as a catspaw, to produce a unified system for a number of people whose loyalties and motivations are different. If it would benefit the business for them to work more closely together, this should be made clear by a suitable re-organisation *first*. (If you happen to be a managing director, please do not try to use computers as a way to make your managers co-operate: make them want to co-operate first, then offer computers as a method for doing so.)

In the BOAC (now BA, Overseas Division) BOADICEA project, the computer expenditure was justified solely on the hard savings in avoiding extra clerical staff dealing with the public. But the equipment, programs, and data needed for this purpose were able to help many other operations at comparatively little incremental cost, such as marketing, scheduling, departure control, flight planning and so on.

But we must return to the uses to be made of our less sophisticated sales accounting system, SALE01.

Lastly, the customer file can be made available to the clerks through enquiry terminals, all through the week. The computer will then have a small 'time-sharing' partition always devoted to actioning requests for customer information from cash clerks, even while other programs are running (see Fig. 54).

This arrangement is likely to be more expensive than the microfiche system described earlier, since terminals cost at least £1000 as against microfiche viewers at £100 or so. The cost of allocating central processor time and space is also considerable, and the designer must think about what

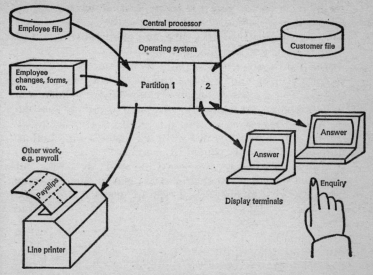

Fig. 54 *Computer with partition permanently allocated for on-line interrogation of a file*

alternative system can be introduced if the computer broke down. Microfiche is less critical from this point of view. However, there are two big advantages in the on-line system:

(a) The program can work out where any customer's information is and retrieve it, e.g. when the clerk keys in THOMAS (or even T, in which case the program will send a list of all customers and their addresses if their name begins with T, and the clerk selects the one required by entering the line number. Anyone who has been to a Chinese restaurant will know why this is called the 'menu' method of selecting which information you want retrieved). With the program to help, it is easier to get the record you want than with microfiche.

(b) If the cash clerk decides that the payment sent by the customer is correct, and clears invoices 8, 10 and 13, he can use his terminal there and then to enter details of payment and the invoices cleared, effectively by-passing the conventional process of card punching, etc.

Generally speaking the customer record will not be altered, even so, at this stage, since various checks against error or fraud must be carried out, and a reconciliation of changes to customer accounts must be made with the incoming payments. There would be some obvious drawbacks if a clerk could clear a customer's indebtedness by simply pressing a few keys at the terminal.

In this case we have a system characterised by *two* response times—a relatively slow, weekly cycle for reacting to input by changing the information on file and by printing invoices, and a fast cycle providing certain information quickly (but not necessarily allowing it to be changed). It will also be apparent that the customer records (or summaries of them) will need to be held on *discs* rather than *tapes*, and the computer program, with the help of the operating system, will need to find individual customers' records on the discs, by converting their name or code number into positioning commands to the read heads, to go to the right disc surface and track. (See Chapter 2 for techniques of handling several 'typewriter' terminals, and for extracting information from discs.)

Credit cards

Many readers will be familiar with credit card systems like Access and Barclaycard, which are based on the 'balance forward' method. Because each item on the monthly statement is supported by a signed voucher for the amount involved, there is less chance of a dispute, and since interest is charged on the balance still unpaid after a month, and partial payments are allowed, the 'open item' method would be impractical. The vouchers produced by the shopkeeper have our code numbers imprinted on them, and the fount in which the figures are embossed on our cards is chosen to be easily readable by an optical document reader. From the shopkeepers' point of view credit cards encourage purchasers, cut down the risk of a till full of cash attracting thieves, and remove the worry of debt collection. The credit card company gets a commission from the shopkeepers, or charges the card-holder. (A drawback at the national level is that credit cards boost inflation by increasing consumer spending power.) The optimum cycle—taking into consideration postage, customers' own likely ability to pay, etc. —for credit card companies is the calendar month. Yet the Access and Barclaycard computers are busy throughout the month by 'cyclical billing'—staggering the dates on which statements are printed. However, access to credit worthiness of individual card-holders must be very rapid—as with our hypothetical journey-planning system. The public, in the persons of shopkeepers, can telephone in this case to check the card-holder's account. Accordingly the basically slow response of such systems is improved by a fast response access system using on-line interrogation terminals, or microfilm/microfiche viewers (see Figs. 53 and 54).

Public utilities billing

Like the credit card companies, the gas, electricity, telephone and rating authorities have a very large customer file. Unlike them, they have a monopoly of the service they supply and in general the customer has little choice but to pay up or be cut off.

Because of the high volume of business, big savings can

be made in clerical costs if the cheapest possible methods are used to record how much of the product each customer has taken. Our telephone bills are calculated semi-automatically from the number of dialled units clocked up: electricity and gas from meter reading cards filled in by hand but read directly by the computer using mark-sensing. Most people regard bills of this kind as 'acts of God' which they sometimes rightly feel are not designed to be checked easily by the customer.

Public utilities can usually raise money cheaply and are not so concerned as other companies about rapid payment. One may see how the objectives of the overall system, as viewed by the chairman of such a utility, is reflected in the attitude it takes to debt collection. He wishes his annual accounts to show a low cost and high profit figure per unit of product sold, and is not so worried about bank overdrafts. Accordingly such utilities invoice at minimum cost, but do not devote a proportionate amount of effort to getting paid. In this they are helped by the average conscientious householder who, unlike a sophisticated businessman, tends to pay off debts when asked to, and certainly when a 'red frightener' comes. (It is amusing to note that it is in some cases cheaper to print the reminders and 'frighteners' as additional copies of the original invoice and throw them away if not needed, than to print them specially when the original invoice is not paid.)

A typical system for public utility billing would be to store customer records on reels of magnetic tape, and to scan this file every day. Customer records will be selected for attention if there is some action to be done:

(a) A meter card to be printed, on a set day of the month, depending (say) on first letter of surname, or, more likely, on street and district,

(b) A statement/invoice to be produced at a pre-determined interval after the meter card was printed,

(c) Reminders and 'frighteners' at further pre-determined intervals if cash is not forthcoming,
(d) Changes in customer information,
(e) Cash receipts,
(f) Other transactions, like customer purchases of equipment, fitting charges, etc., hire purchase.

Each of these actions, or *trans*actions, may involve a large program to cover the complicated logic required: so much so that the total number of lines in the program (roughly related to the number of instructions) may be over 100 000. As we saw in Chapter 2, information about customers is obviously too voluminous to store in the central processor's expensive memory, and will be stored on tape or disc. We also saw that programs when not in use can be stored in a 'library' on disc. In the case of very large programs, we can arrange for a nucleus, responsible for deciding which transactions have to be dealt with at any moment, to be resident in the central processor's memory throughout the reading of the magnetic tape, and for only the more frequently used subordinate programs (e.g. 'CASH-RECEIVED PROCEDURE') to be in central memory as well: most of the subordinate programs will only be loaded from the library when a transaction of the corresponding type has been found (e.g. 'DEFAULTING-HP-PAYMENT').

It is the analyst's responsibility to recommend how much central processor memory should be bought to minimise the costs of the run: too much will be expensive, too little will mean that the run will be slowed up while programs are constantly being loaded from the library.

We could of course sort the transactions so that all CASH-RECEIVED transactions were done first, then INVOICES, and so on. But this would mean many passes of the magnetic tapes, and could slow the procedure up. An answer to this is to do a preliminary pass of the main customer file, during which all customer records which are

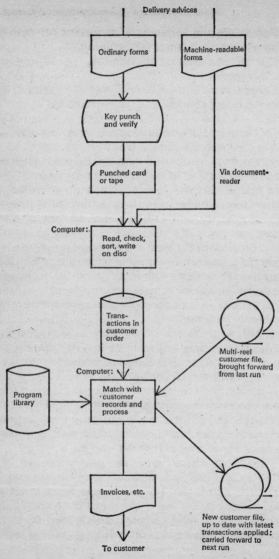

Fig. 55 *Processing a large customer file with a large program partly in memory and partly on disc*

involved in *any* transaction are extracted and copied on to some working file, tape or disc: this will be only a fraction of the size of the original file, and can be read several times by the central processor, each time with a limited amount of particular transaction-processing programs in its memory, which will add their results to the working file.

Finally, we can read the whole customer file again, and copy it out plus the results obtained from the working file, to make up the new customer file.

A refinement of this technique is illustrated below: the customer file is not re-created *every* day, but yesterday's working tape results are included in the initial extraction run, and customer records from this file, which are of course more up to date, are taken in preference to the main, multi-reel file (see Fig. 56).

It must, however, be said that the trend is towards the single pass approach, because methods of loading programs efficiently from disc are now very sophisticated and included in the services provided by the operating system. This is a major feature of the IBM/370 range sold with 'virtual memory', where the programmers and analysts can write systems that imply the central processor has much more actual memory than it has. When an instruction is reached which is in the library rather than in memory, the operating system, assisted by special circuitry, automatically retrieves a new 'page' or program from the disc library, containing the instruction required.

It must be pointed out that this does not mean the analyst can recommend the purchase of a machine with almost no memory. The result would be that the performance would be abysmal, since programs would have to be fetched from the disc library far too frequently. (This phenomenon is called 'thrashing'.) The analyst has some powerful techniques at his disposal, but he has to be cautious: to find the most cost-effective solution is difficult. Simulation may be needed to see which approach will work best.

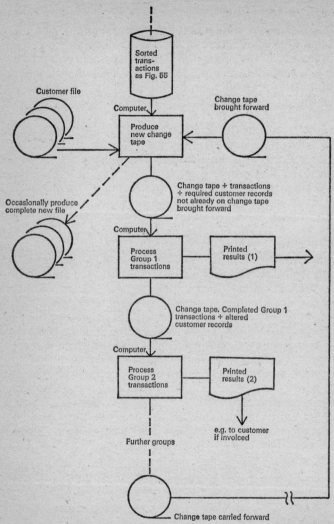

Fig. 56 *Handling a multi-reel file by extracting a change tape, and passing it repeatedly through the computer, dealing with all transactions of a particular group on each pass*

Before leaving public utilities, we note that the enormous volumes of data they handle have given rise to the document readers described before, and in addition, to devices which 'data preparation' operators use to transcribe forms into machine-readable form more efficiently than the simple card or paper tape punches. The operator has a similar keyboard, but sees the results of the key-strokes on a screen, and the actual information is stored on magnetic tape or discs—often 'mini' versions of the big ones on the computer proper, known as cassettes and 'floppy discs' respectively.

Data preparation devices of this kind, which save the cost of punched cards and promote fewer errors and more key strokes per hour, include machines from CMC, Redifon, and Inforex besides the big computer manufacturers. Some of these include a small mini-computer to control the operation. Or, as at Rank Hovis McDougall at Acton, a partition of the main computer itself (ICL System 4) is devoted to collecting information from typewriter terminals much as we described in Fig. 22.

Purchasing

The purchasing manager has to provide goods of the right quantity and quality at exactly the right time, at the minimum price. The first uses of computers in this area were just a mirror-image of sales invoicing: a purchase ledger was held, suppliers' bills added to it, and at the end of the month payments were made. The main objective was to save clerical costs and mistakes. But now computers are applied more widely:

(a) to check suppliers' performance by keeping statistics on under-deliveries, lateness, poor quality, and over-pricing,
(b) to compare suppliers one with another, so as to choose the best in future,

(c)   to delay payment as far as is legal, ethical, and expedient,

(d)   to monitor the progress of critical deliveries through the various steps (the author developed a system 'CHASER' designed for factory use, which was in fact first applied in the purchasing area within the RACAL electronics group).

Once again, the kernel of the purchasing system has a medium response time geared to the accountants' schedules, but connected to it may be the slow-response systems used for long-term decisions about suppliers, and fast-response systems for controlling critical deliveries. This last is of great importance to motor manufacturers, who keep stocks of components like windscreen wipers to a minimum, but order them in bulk from suppliers and 'call off' deliveries fairly frequently to feed the assembly line. A mistake or delay in the arrival of a consignment could halt the line and cost a great deal. Accordingly clerks called 'parts analysts' keep track of these deliveries, in many cases (as at Ford Motor Company) using terminals to obtain information on demand, stocks, and expected consignments.

The purchasing department, which places orders on behalf of other departments in the firm, and the accounts department, which actually *pays* suppliers, should be kept apart for reasons of security. A purchasing clerk, for example, could set up a friend as a bogus supplier and arrange for another friend in accounts to pay bills sent in by him for goods not actually delivered. Accordingly a good analyst will invite an auditor to go over a proposed new system in this area very carefully, to ensure that it discourages such frauds, and does not actually offer new possibilities within the computer department itself: could an operator, with a programmer's help, add a bogus supplier to the file and divert payments to it that should go against real suppliers' invoices? Could valid discounts be omitted, so that a real but crooked supplier is paid too much, and the proceeds are split?

Purchasing professionals often feel that the rest of the company regards them as awarding contracts to the supplier who sends them most whisky at Christmas, and acting as dogs in the manger when something is wanted quickly from a named, new supplier. The analyst can help to combat this unfair image, improve the service they offer, and tighten security. Incidentally, computers often print out pre-signed cheques—an apparently hair-raising procedure, but in practice less liable to fraud than some of the less obvious parts of the system like discounts and contracts.

Purchasing procedures fall into two main parts, one the responsibility of the purchasing department itself, and the other of accounts (see Fig. 57 (*a*) and (*b*)).

If a department needs some goods, for example steel to build a ship, they send a requisition to the purchasing department giving details of their needs; type, quantity and quality of goods, date required, and in many cases the product or project for which the goods are needed. This latter information enables the system to calculate how much is being spent on each, and this can be compared against budget.

The purchasing department is responsible for meeting the requisition, but at the lowest cost to the organisation. A supplier is selected who is reliable, and whose prices or discounts are most attractive. Often a supplier or two suppliers are nominated for a particular type of goods, and changed only when they let us down or a new supplier with better/cheaper goods appears. The computer system can help by monitoring suppliers' performance as follows:

Delivery on time, e.g. % of occasions late

Quality, e.g. % of deliveries sent back because of faults

Price, e.g. average price each, based on normal quantity deliveries

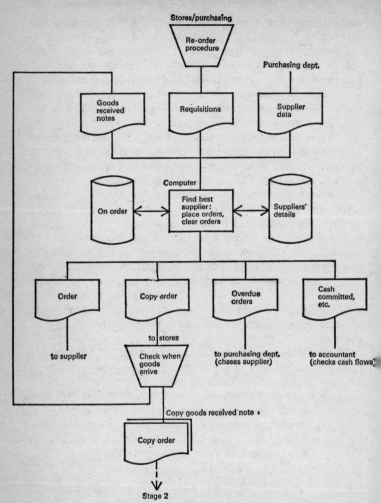

Fig. 57(a) *Stage 1: Ordering, progressing, and maintaining supplies records*

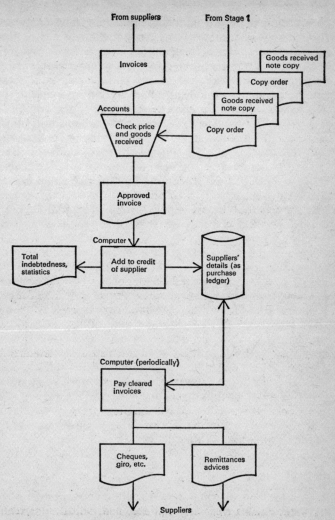

Fig. 57(b) *Stage 2: Payments*

In addition there are unquantifiables like 'how likely are they to stay in business?' The computer might not be suspicious if their prices are half anyone else's, but we should be.

Statistics are thus collected by the regular computer runs on what the Americans call 'vendor performance', and these can be tabulated periodically and used by purchasing to decide who should be chosen. Accordingly the computer system will be regularly run with coded requisition information and supplier details. The advantage of running not *too* frequently is that several small orders can be bulked together for the same supplier, and thus save on delivery charges, postage, and discounts. In this case some urgent requisitions may have to be allowed to bypass the system and be sent out before going through the computer, in which case the computer-printed order form is just an official confirmation.

The computer will produce the orders to be sent to suppliers, lumping together several order items where possible to save postage, and also send copies back to the requisitioning departments, to tell them the order has gone, and for the department to return when the goods are delivered. At this stage the computer will add the new orders against the supplier's record on file, and check whether any old orders are likely to run late. If so, it can print out automatically a letter to the supplier asking when the orders will come and why they have been delayed. It can also print a schedule of expected cash commitments incurred as a result of the orders placed, so that the accountants can make sure there will be enough money in the bank to cover the cheques to be written a month or so after delivery.

Payroll

This is the 'classic' computer task, often chosen in the early days because its rules are well specified, and it runs regularly: apparently just the job for the computer department to cut its teeth on. Unfortunately the benefits from using a computer for producing payslips are low: in the normal company the possibility of reducing the number of clerks is small, and there are no obvious other reductions in costs. Only when there is a large work-force paid according to complicated rules by a large centralised office, is there much chance of a computer system for payroll making a profit— as with the armed forces, or miners. In other cases one is liable to end up with a team of computer payroll analysts and programmers at least as big as and better paid than, the clerks the system displaces, if any. If one has a computer with spare capacity it is reasonable to put payroll on, but almost certainly by using a 'package' as supplied by specialists such as COMPAY or UNIPAY, whose programs take care of the intricacies of tax and National Insurance. The Westminster Bank offers such a service also. One's *own* analysts and programmers should be working on systems which can improve revenue and cash flow, and reduce costs, in the areas of sales, distribution, production, and planning: payroll is a chore which has to be done, but it is not particularly beneficial to have it done perfectly rather than adequately.

One may, however, argue that the information used by the payroll programs is about a resource of crucial importance to the organisation: that is, the human beings who make it succeed by their skills and efforts. Moreover the payroll system may be triggered by information on attendance and on the start and end of particular pieces of work, particularly in the case of performance bonus payments. In this case we may find it worthwhile adding our own special programs to the 'front' and 'back' of the payroll system itself (see Fig. 58).

Once again we can see the pattern—a regular, comparatively dull (with due deference to the accountants) and, in comparison with revenue collection, unimprovable book-keeping operation turns out to be the basis for manpower

planning (slow-response, strategic) and production progress
control (rapid-response, tactical).

Information likely to be present on employee record:

Name
Address
Staff number and department
Sex, date of birth, date of joining
Marital status
Wage rate(s)
Bonus rate(s)
Category (e.g. fitter)
Tax code
Gross pay to date
Tax to date
Pensions to date
Deductions
Holiday entitlement
Qualifications
Salary and job history
Promotion prospects

Stock control

For a company, holding stock is both a good and a bad
thing. If plenty of *raw materials* are kept, there is little
chance of customers' orders being delivered late or of
machines and men standing idle because the materials were
not there. If plenty of *finished stocks* are kept, sudden
demands from customers can be met immediately. If *part-
finished* goods are held, especially if they are sub-assemblies
that are common to several finished product lines, we can
allocate them to be assembled to meet customer orders.
British Oxygen's welding division markets many types of
welding equipment, but several types will make use of the

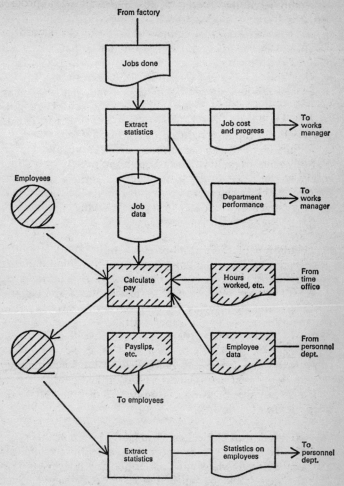

Fig. 58 *Payroll system (shaded), with additions*

same sub-assembly—a control device, or cutting head—and this can be kept in stock and used on whichever finished product is in demand. In times of material shortages and inflation, a company could well do better to have its assets in the form of goods rather than in cash. Also, buying or making things in small quantities is uneconomic. But the other side of the coin is that materials can rust, be stolen, become obsolete, and invariably take up room. Their purchase costs have reduced the company's cash (or increased its overdraft) and also reduced its freedom of action.

For any company, in a given economic climate and a given market demand, there will be an optimum policy for holding stocks at the three levels—raw material, finished, and part-finished stocks. American companies pay particular attention to 'inventory' as they term stocks, and the level of inventory across US industry is used as an economic indicator.

Calculation of the optimum stock policy is definitely a slow-response, management-science type of computer job, and simulation as described in the last chapter is particularly useful. (The level of stock can be regarded as a 'queue' at a GPO counter: deliveries of material are 'arrivals', and the manufacturing or customer off-take is like the queue-reducing activity of the GPO clerk.) But as well as establishing targets for the levels of each kind of stock to be held, there is another bread-and-butter job to be done, actually recording the charges: issues, receipts, adjustments.

The advantages of using a computer to do this dull book-keeping are as follows:

(a) Reduction in clerical costs (usually insignificant).
(b) Faster response to inventory movements: accountants are pleased when raw materials are converted into finished stock, or finished stock into deliveries, since they then appear in the books at a higher value.
(c) Faster response to deviations from the targets pre-

established, so that dangerously low stocks will be re-ordered, and obsolete stock disposed of.

(d) Automatic supply of information to Production and Sales on the availability of materials and products.

(e) Statistics about demand, usage, costs which can be used periodically to change the targets worked out by the strategic, slow-response system.

You may find it interesting to do a small simulation yourself showing how good stock control can benefit a company. Let us suppose we have to manage a stock of spare engines for tractors, each engine costing £100. We can sell these at £150, but they cost £2 per month each to hold. Moreover for every shipment of engines we order, there is a flat rate of £100 to cover administration and handling costs. We can assume delivery is instantaneous (though in practice it will take one or more months). Demand is variable but the average level is 10 units a month.

Our starting stock is 15 engines. We have to decide two main questions—how few engines do we allow to be in stock before re-ordering, and what is the minimum number we re-order when the number falls below this level?

Let us start by *guessing* these figures, at 10 in each case.

Now we can draw up a 'bin card' for these engines (Fig. 59):

Month	On hand	Issued	Received	Ordered	Costs £	Revenue £
Engines: Minimum Re-order Quantity: 10. Re-order Level: 10						
1	15		0			
2						
3						
4						
5						
6						
7						
8						
9						
10						
				TOTALS:		

Fig. 59 *Stock control bin card*

We need to set out the proposed processing rules as a logic block diagram (see Fig. 60).

To try out this procedure, with the assumed figures for re-order quantity and re-order level, we need some typical demand values. (I obtained the ones that follow by writing a short program which generated random numbers in the range 0 to .999 . . ., and applied these to a procedure for selecting a corresponding demand level, with a Poisson distribution, average 10.)

12	i.e. in month	1 we receive orders for 12 engines
8	,, ,, 2 ,,	,, ,, ,, 8 ,,
14	.	
13	.	
9	etc.	
13	.	
12	.	
6	.	
13	. .	
16	.	

(The average of these few values is in fact 11.6—not 10, which is reached only after a long enough run.)

We now cycle through the logic diagram in Fig. 60. In month 1, nothing need be done at block A. B refers us to demand value 1, i.e. 12. At C demand is less than on-hand, so remains at 12. In block D we reduce on-hand to 3 and credit revenue with 12 × £150 = £1800. In E we write the new balance on-hand 3 in month 2, and decide to order 10 for next month. In F we find the holding cost this month to be:

$$\frac{(15 + 3)}{2} \times £2 = £18$$

In month 2 we note (block A) the arrival of the 10 ordered, and their cost, 10 × £100 + £100, and continue as before, and continue similarly with the remaining months.

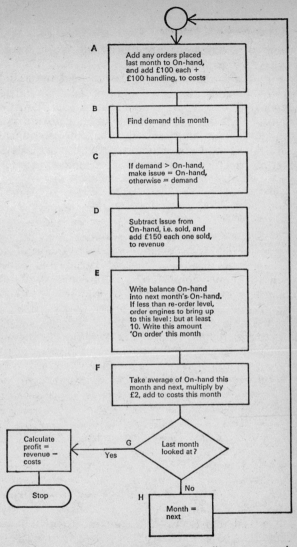

A Add any orders placed last month to On-hand, and add £100 each + £100 handling, to costs

B Find demand this month

C If demand > On-hand, make issue = On-hand, otherwise = demand

D Subtract issue from On-hand, i.e. sold, and add £150 each one sold, to revenue

E Write balance On-hand into next month's On-hand. If less than re-order level, order engines to bring up to this level: but at least 10. Write this amount 'On order' this month

F Take average of On-hand this month and next, multiply by £2, add to costs this month

G Last month looked at?

Yes — Calculate profit = revenue — costs

Stop

No

H Month = next

Fig. 60 *Stock accounting logic block diagram: example*

The bin card now looks like that in Fig. 61 (like Fig. 59 with extra numbers).

Perhaps you would like to calculate through to the end of month 10, acting the part of a computer and using the block diagram in Fig. 60 as your program. Check your results with Appendix 6. We have been doing straightforward book-keeping, and a computer version of our efforts could save clerical costs and, if run promptly, could avoid delays in re-ordering which could mean we were sometimes short of stock to meet demand later on.

But we can also *analyse* the results of the ten months of activity, to *revise* the figures of 're-order quantity 10' and 're-order level 10', and so increase revenue and/or reduce costs, through the use of a more sophisticated program. It looks as though we have kept ourselves too short of stock and thus had to turn away demands, losing the value of 11 sales. If the ten months are typical, demand is at least 10 a month on average, so that the re-order level of 10 is too low. Moreover, when an order is placed, it may be cheaper to obtain a larger quantity, say 15, and keep the surplus a month at £2 each, holding cost, and avoid the £100 administrative cost of placing a further order. The mathematical techniques for calculating the optimum values will not be dealt with here but can be looked up in textbooks on stock control and operational research. Let us regard them as a 'black box' in this context.

But it would not be sensible to revise our re-order level and minimum quantity every time we had a demand, since such calculations must be based on a reasonably large statistical sample. Hence it is argued that stock recording is a 'medium-response' system with a 'slow-response' system gradually adjusting some of the factors used by the medium-response system. This notion of a hierarchy of control systems at different logical and temporal levels is part of cybernetics and control theory.

For administrative convenience we can build our slow-

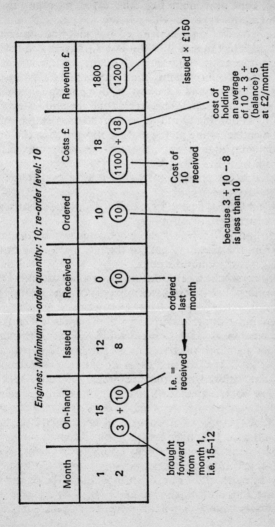

Fig. 61 *Bin card after second month*

response control system into the same program as the medium-response system, and activate it at periodic intervals rather as SALE01 only performed invoices and statements when it detected that it was the last Friday in the month. Another approach is to go through *all* the calculations at the shorter interval but to 'damp' the changes that are computed so as to avoid too quick reactions to demand changes which are probably random. This technique is known as 'exponential smoothing', and is rather like working out a moving average, while giving extra importance to the more recent demand figures since these presumably may reflect new trends.

As noted, stock control is divisible into several areas:

(a) raw materials, where 'demand' is from the factory and 're-orders' are on suppliers,
(b) part-finished stock, or sub-assemblies, where 'demand' is from the assembly part of the factory, and re-orders are on raw material stocks,
(c) finished stock, where 'demand' is from customers and 're-orders' are on the assembly part of the factory.

In the example quoted, demand was assumed to be from outside customers and unpredictable except statistically from past demand or by market surveys (see previous chapter). But in the two first cases we can *calculate* demand by working back from the customers' demand. If ten engines are wanted, then forty sparking plugs will be needed: if we make sparking plugs each requiring two washers bought from a supplier, then we will need eighty washers. (As a matter of fact it is actually sometimes easier *not* to make use of this knowledge because of the extensive calculations needed: also the fact that small items like washers are used in many places and can most easily be controlled by just meeting the demands made by the factory as if they were unpredictable.)

It is also apparent that the three areas of stock control are intimately connected with

(a) purchasing (discussed earlier)
(b) production control (to be discussed next)
(c) sales order processing (next chapter)

respectively. Please refer back to Fig. 57. The purchase *requisitions* mentioned there are none other than the re-orders which the stock control system produces. If both systems are on the computer, we can *integrate* these aspects (see Fig. 62).
Note that in the schematic, the existence of two 'computer processing' boxes does not imply two computers. In fact we

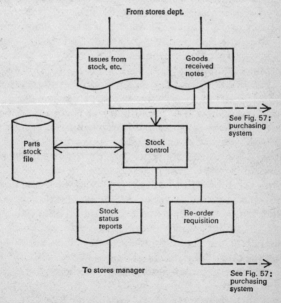

Fig. 62 *How stock control system links with purchasing system*

could well conflate both systems into a single program if their mutual cycle times were compatible.

Stock control, and production control (next section) are very sensitive areas in a company. Political battles can rage round such questions as what level of demand should we be able to meet, and who (e.g. production, accounts, or sales) should say how much investment should be made in stock. Stock policy affects everyone in the business and may decide whether the business succeeds or fails. The consequence is that unlike payroll—a low-return, low-risk, well-demarcated computer application—stock control offers big benefits, is risky to everyone's reputation, and involves all the important officers of the business. It should be first on the list of jobs to do, for a systems analyst! But he must ensure that he has the proper sponsorship and that all the managers concerned have agreed the basic assumptions and corporate targets of the new system, and that their views can be incorporated in the design, and that there exists a sensible way to resolve differences of view if this becomes necessary.

He may need to gain his sponsors' confidence by installing a successful system before he is given free rein in the field of stock control. If this preliminary is necessary, an operational 'sharp-end' system like purchasing is a good one to begin with because it leads nicely into stock control, and introduces him to its concepts and the right people in the organisation.

There are many proprietary packages in stock control, because like payroll both the mathematics and the book-keeping can be quite involved and yet are common to most businesses, unlike sales accounting. (A firm making super-tankers and one making juke boxes have quite similar problems controlling stocks of rivets, wire, nuts and bolts, and sheet metal, but their invoices are likely to have very little in common.)

Most proprietary packages are coupled with a related

application, e.g. ICL NIMMS is production control oriented but includes a stock control element: IBM IMPACT was aimed at the distributive trades with emphasis on finished stocks.

A practical problem in setting up any computer-based stock control system is the introduction of a unique identification system for individual stock items. This problem actually exists in a non-computer system but is not recognised: we perhaps keep the same kind of washer under three different names for many years and not until the computer system is introduced do we find this out: and the discovery is well worth making, since it will save expense in holding, ordering, and recording stock. One of the biggest stock control systems in the world is that of the USAF, and they have a continuous exercise to track down and eliminate aliases, i.e. different names for the same part.

The actual identifier for a part is worth careful design. Its English description is usually ambiguous and long winded, like WILLOW PATTERN LARGE TEAPOT. In some cases we may think of a code which describes the part: Fords used a twenty-two digit and letter code for car spares which in theory could tell you what car, what year, which system (electrical, exhaust . . .) the part fitted. But for computer use this was replaced by a 'meaningless' but neat, short, six digit number. To guard against mistakes we can add an extra digit to all part numbers which is calculated from the others in such a way that whenever the computer system receives an alleged part number, it will recalculate this 'check digit' and reject any that show that there must have been an error in copying. So in our sales accounting program, the identifier 'LARGE TEAPOT' could be replaced within the system by a code such as 123–5.

Production control

Typically, a factory receives raw materials or parts from its suppliers, makes other parts, and assembles parts together into sub-assemblies, and sub-assemblies into finished products for sale. Of course there are other modes of production as in oil refineries, with their own special systems, but the mode described is a very common one, and occurs in businesses making anything from pianos to Concordes.

Suppose we have a business selling toy carts and toy wheelbarrows (see Fig. 63).

Now it will make sense to make and buy only one kind of Box and Wheel, because we can then divert supplies of these items to whichever product is most in demand. Let us suppose our finished stock control system issues us with instructions to make 500 W's and 200 C's. There is a straightforward calculation to be done: we will need

$$(500 \times 1) + (200 \times 1) \text{ Boxes to make}$$
$$(500 \times 1) + (200 \times 4) \text{ Wheels to buy}$$

With many products and many parts, we could well use a computer to 'explode' a proposed schedule of manufacture into parts requirements, and all we need is a file which gives a list of parts for each product, and a program to multiply and add up (see Fig. 64).

This would certainly relieve us of a tedious calculation job. But it does not answer two important questions—*when* should the parts be made available, and are there some sub-assemblies or parts already in stock, so that we do not need to make or buy *all* the parts implied by the exploded manufacturing schedule? If the system ignores these questions we shall either have to do a clerical operation to date-stamp, or reduce the quantity on, the Parts Needed forms coming out of the computer in Fig. 64. But the computer can cope with this refinement, and does so by:

(a) applying standard manufacture/assembly/supply lead-times to each level of product structure. Please refer back to Fig. 39: by the use of such a network the computer can work out that if the schedule for W's is

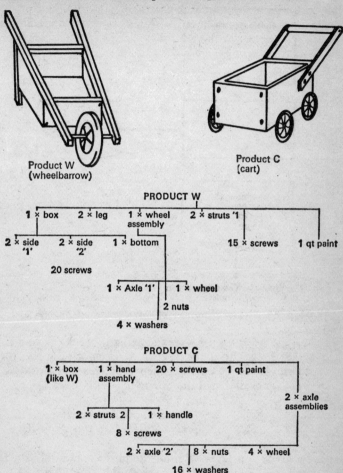

Fig. 63 *Product structures*
The two products have two components in common: the wheel and the box

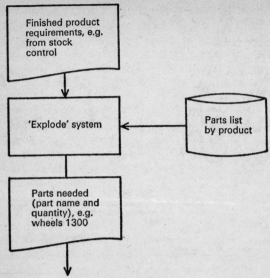

Fig. 64 *Simple 'explosion' of manufacturing schedule*

50 per week for 10 weeks starting in week 30, and it takes 1 week to paint, 1 week to assemble, 2 weeks to assemble the boxes . . ., then the Sides and Bottoms must be available at the rate of:

$$\left. \begin{array}{l} 2 \times 50 \times \text{Side '1's} \\ 2 \times 50 \times \text{Side '2's} \\ 1 \times 50 \times \text{Bottoms} \end{array} \right\} \begin{array}{l} \text{for each of 10 weeks starting in} \\ \text{week } (30 - 1 - 1 - 2) = 26 \end{array}$$

(b) with the top level assembly requirements established and after consolidating requirements for W's and C's where they are for a common assembly, the computer can scan the stock control file and see if there is already enough of these assemblies in stores, or on order, to meet the timetable without further work: or whether some or all of them must be produced. When the balance required has been found, the computer must carry out (a) again at this lower level, and repeat (b) again, and so on until the lowest level parts—i.e. bought ones—are reached.

This procedure is called a 'level by level explosion with netting off against stock'. Instead of a straight list of components per product type which was all that was needed in the simple system of Fig. 64, it needs a 'product structure file' which covers the various levels and *intermediate* subassemblies. It also needs to refer to the stock file at each level, and to allocate stock planned to be there on the date in question, or else to raise requisitions. You can, therefore, appreciate that production control and stock control go hand in hand (see Fig. 65).

So far we have described a system which will be of considerable use to the factory manager, purchasing manager, and sales manager. But we have made use of rather broad-brush *planning* estimates (e.g. two weeks to assemble boxes). In fact, an operative probably assembles a given box in about five minutes flat, and we allow two weeks to take account of the fact that he probably works on big batches of boxes. The two weeks include getting the sides, bottoms, and screws out of stores, setting up jigs and getting screwdrivers, assembling the whole batch, putting the finished boxes back into stores, and adding on a good allowance for illness, repairs, shortages and administrative delays. But the production manager would welcome help in the detailed hour by hour allocation of operations on individual batches of work to his operatives and machines, usually grouped in 'shops' each specialising in one type of process—painting, assembly, etc.

Accordingly the final output of the system described so far may enter a further system—*machine-shop loading* or

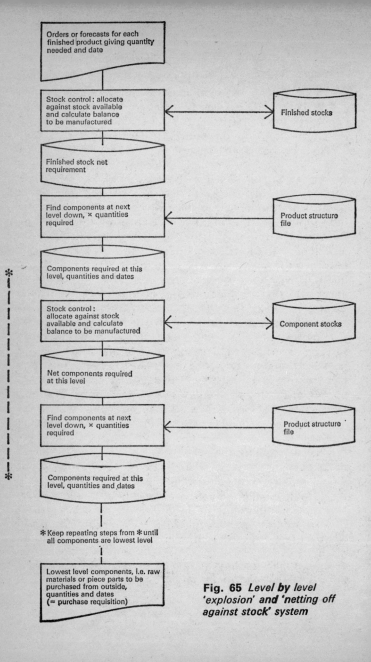

Fig. 65 *Level by level 'explosion' and 'netting off against stock' system*

scheduling, which takes the requirements with their crude *weekly* planning dates, and tries to fit them into an *hour by hour* schedule of small batches which can be done on time, and efficiently, by the operatives.

Nobody knows a way to do this quickly and with guaranteed optimum results. There are billions of ways of scheduling a fair-sized set of jobs on to a fair-sized set of machine shops. However, there are some reasonable rules of thumb: after all, production controllers manage to devise workable schedules. One way is to load the shops as late as possible while still ensuring each job emerges by its externally imposed completion day, then to move the jobs earlier in time in such a way that the shops have an even load. This is called 'backward scheduling to infinite capacity, followed by forward scheduling to finite capacity'. If the results are not perfect, various tricks like breaking the jobs into smaller jobs to be run in parallel on different machines can be tried. Such a system is IBM CAPOSS.

In ICL NIMMS, the scheduling system can use a variety of techniques including PERT, as mentioned earlier. At the UKAE, it was recognised that the problem of loading shops and scheduling is mathematically similar—oddly enough— to that of designing printed circuit board layouts, and a production control package WASP was the result. At the AWRE a simple system called SWORD has also been developed. Honeywell's FACTOR includes scheduling, but as part of an overall manufacturing control package which covers stock control, product structure files, and purchasing.

As the scope of computer-based production control is extended into the hour by hour operations, we find a worrying thing happening. Firstly, the computations get more time consuming, because it is really one of the hardest problems (as hard, for example, as chess-playing) a computer can tackle, and secondly, the results can be invalidated by an operative not turning up or a machine breaking down: then the whole elaborate plan, based on getting optimum performance out of the factory over a week, is thrown out and must be recalculated, as it must if an operation took too long, or a job has to be repeated because of an operative error.

For these reasons many computer-based scheduling systems are only *simulators*: they may be run weekly like a typical medium-response system, and their results are probably invalid, at the detailed level, even before the schedule reaches the factory. But if the schedule shows a reasonable margin of spare capacity the production controller will accept the set of jobs to be done this week—then, in all probability, schedule them in a different way, in the light of his own knowledge, and being well aware he will have to change tactics several times during the week. We are faced here with the paradox that optimum solutions may take so long to work out, and be so expensive to work out more frequently than weekly, that the data on which they are based will be obsolete and the solution therefore invalid, or very likely *not* optimum.

For this reason efforts are made to get information from the factory quickly, within minutes of a machine breaking down or a job being completed. There are many *data collection systems* available, where the operative or foreman records the completion of a job, or any other significant event, by recording it at a special terminal designed for industrial use (i.e. resistant to oil, impact, and over-enthusiastic operation) and directly coupled to a mini-computer which controls several such terminals and produces the information in computer-readable form ready for a daily or hourly production control run. An early shop-floor data collection system was designed by IBM for Boeing: the IBM 357.

It is even better to wire up the machine-tool itself to record its activities, as in the Dextralog System developed by Terminal Display Systems with NRDC backing. However, some information may be necessarily provided by the human operator, such as his own employee number.

This aspect of production control is called progress recording and is the vital feed-back needed to make the computer-based system credible and efficient. No production controller will have much time for a beautiful solution which ignores the fact that the paint shop caught fire this morning: he would sooner have a workable, if inelegant new schedule which can keep things going while he telephones round for some paint-shop capacity outside. A number of very rapid turn-round production control systems have been developed to this philosophy which should perhaps be called rapid-response rather than medium-response, and dealt with in Chapter 5. However, we can note them here:

JOBMAN (Honeywell)
CHASER (REDAC)

(An interest should be declared here: the latter system is one developed jointly by REDAC Ltd. and the author.)

We can see now how the systems discussed in this chapter start to link up. Purchasing deals with the bought-out requirements identified by stock control: production control deals with the made-in requirements, and works alternately with stock control when doing the 'Explosion level by level with netting off' operation. Production control requires feedback from the shop floor about operatives' activities, and this same information, especially when bonus is paid, feeds into the payroll system. The sales accounting system uses the (finished) stock control's product file for invoicing. We shall see how one can deliberately plan for these systems to complement each other in Chapter 6 (Data bases).

Miscellaneous medium-response systems

There are some other systems we should mention briefly besides the big ones covered above:

Management Accounting. This mechanism tells us if any manager, department, project, or supplier is costing us more or providing less revenue than we expected. In a small organisation, the managing director can often see for himself if things are off target: in a large one with many levels of management and many products, good variances can hide bad, and a formal system has to be used. A computer-based management accounting system accepts information from the preceding 'operational systems' and summarises the results so that individuals' performances (e.g. the purchase manager's in avoiding supply delays) can be expressed in figures, using money to bring to the same measure different responsibilities.

Financial Accounting. This covers the 'real money' that the firm spends and gets, depreciation, tax, etc. In a small business the totals that appear on reports from the various systems already described will be collected and will eventually appear in the annual accounts by orthodox accounting procedures. A computer-based system can automate this process for large corporations with many divisions.

Share Register. A computer-based system can maintain a list of all shareholders and do the paperwork to issue dividends, scrip issues, circulars, etc. There are several packages available.

Capital Assets. A record for each capital item (filing cabinets, cars, etc.) is kept and its cost, depreciation, location, etc. recorded for accounting and control purposes.

Human Resource Accounting, or *Skills Inventory.* A computer system in this area is logical enough but may be repugnant to the liberal mind. It is attractive to keep records of one's employees and their qualifications, performance, etc. so that they can be promoted, selected for new projects, praised, or given remedial training (euphemism for 'blamed'), using computer-based information probably stored on the same tape or disc as the payroll employee file. This is an exceptionally touchy subject and will be discussed in Chapter 7.

5

Rapid-response Computer-based Systems

Even in those systems described in Chapters 3 and 4 as
basically slow- and medium-response, we saw how a rapid-
response 'annexe' to the system might be added to cover
one aspect of them, as in the case where sales accounting,
basically a weekly or monthly operation, might include
provision for quick access to customer indebtedness data
for credit control and for cash posting.

But we now consider systems which are *basically* rapid-
response: where the human part of the system relies on the
computer to contribute its part within a timescale of a few
seconds. We shall examine in particular:

> Reservations
> Banking
> Point of sale
> Information retrieval—police

Reservations

This is the classic rapid-response computer-based system,
and was pioneered by US airline systems such as SABRE
and PANAMAC. The economic reasons for introducing
such systems can be summarised as follows:

> The high value of filling an aircraft seat which would
> otherwise have remained empty,
> The high cost of protracted booking procedures in terms
> of wasted clerical time and traveller irritation.

Rapid-response systems tend to be expensive, because of the extra equipment needed to cover peak loads and possible failures. Consequently, when applied to stock control (which is all that an airline reservations system is) the value of the stock items must be proportionately high. A seat on a long-haul airline, if filled, will bring in from £50 to £500 in extra revenue, so that spending say £1 in computer support at the booking stage is worthwhile if it raises the chance of filling the seat by only a modest amount.

The BEACON system of BEA (before the formation of British Airways) was particularly creditable in that it showed a profit even though the average seat revenue is much lower for *short*-haul airlines. But attempts to use computers for car hire, theatre or hotel bookings have been less successful because the intrinsic value of the transaction is that much lower than aircraft journeys, unless they can 'ride on the back' of another such system. One can, for example, make hotel reservations through British Airways' BABS system, as a by-product of the seat reservations system.

A rapid-response reservations system fills more seats because the number of seats still available is known more accurately by the booking clerk. Some months before the flight the number of seats booked will be low, and if a revised list is published only every day or two, there is still a very low probability of all the seats suddenly being taken up. But in the last few hours before departure, cancellations and new bookings happen more and more frequently, and if reservations are made on the basis of old lists, many people will be accepted when all the seats have gone, or many turned away when seats have become free.

One possible policy would be to accept everyone regardless, and if too many people turn up, to put up with their indignation. In the USA deliberate 'over-booking' is illegal, and elsewhere the airlines recognise that such a policy will result in disgruntled customers who will have to be placated at considerable expense (hotel rooms, food and drink) and who next time will choose another airline. Accordingly an airline may set its own confidential safety margin and use its computer system to minimise *inadvertent* overbooking, due to delays in bookings being reflected in the availability lists used by booking clerks, or to straight-forward errors.

To turn to the second consideration, clerical costs, we need to visualise the task of a booking clerk. He has to provide a quick service to a business man who has a compli-cated schedule requiring him to be in Seattle on Tuesday morning and Honolulu on Thursday: he then has to re-assure a nervous mother wanting the cheapest way to visit her son in Australia, with vegetarian meals on board, but not minding just when the flight goes. His task involves applied psychology, timetabling, and fare calculation as well as just finding if a seat is free and booking it. He has to find what the customer thinks he wants, formalise it, and sell him on the idea of travelling with this airline. If he asks for one seat, try to persuade him to take his wife too—or how about a stop-over in Florida? The computer then gets to work to find the best way to realise the journey. Perhaps it replies with an 'impossible' indicator, in which case the customer and clerk re-define the journey—he may be willing to post-pone the trip, or travel a different route. There is thus a three-way-interaction, controlled by the booking clerk (if he is competent), which leads to another sale and another satisfied customer. In a typical situation, the interaction may proceed as in Fig. 66.

We can see that we have to study the psychological and ergonomic aspects of this transaction in depth, so that the clerk and his computer assistant work as the ideal team. He must be able to express his ideas quickly to the computer, and will use an abbreviated code, e.g. ENQ for enquiry, or even just Q. The terminal can display information at several hundred characters a second, so he can sometimes specify what he wants to know most efficiently by asking a general

Customer	Clerk	Computer
I need to be in Seattle on Tuesday morning		
	When would you like to travel?	
Overnight, I suppose: on the other hand . . .		
	I'll see what we've got. (Keys in ENQ LHR–SEA 0512 0600–0800: i.e. 'enquiry—London Heathrow to Seattle on 5th December, any time of arrival between 6 and 8 a.m.')	
		ABC128 OVERNIGHT DIRECT NO SEATS ABC391-AA809 OVERNIGHT VIA NY TRANSFER TO AMERICAN AIRLINES
	Or maybe you'd like to have a good night's sleep before starting work (0412 0600–2300: i.e. 'same destination,' day before, arriving 6 a.m. to 11 p.m.')	
		ABC380 DIRECT ARR 1900 LOCAL MONDAY NO SEATS
That's a good thought		
	But you're not the only one with that thought! Are you planning to visit anywhere else? (Clerk is getting worried: will he lose this sale?)	
Yes—I'm going to Honolulu, anytime really, but I thought of going on from Seattle to get there around Thursday		
	I expect you've considered Honolulu first, and *then* on to Seattle?	

and so on, ending we hope with:

Customer	Clerk	Computer
		ABC606 LHR-HLU 1M 0112 CONFIRMED ABC773 HLU-SEA 1M 0412 CONFIRMED ABC336 SEA-LHR 1M 0612 CONFIRMED HOTELS/HIRE CARS OK TICKET COLLECT BY 2511
	Here's a printout of your itinerary	
I'm glad I thought of going the other way round. Thanks for your help		

Fig. 66 *Two humans and a computer solve a travel problem*

question, and indicating which of a number of possibilities he is interested in. E.g. Fig. 67.

Let us see how these systems requirements are met. First, we need a fast, reliable terminal with a keyboard that may well have special function keys to suit the airline (or some

Clerk	Computer
Q HOTEL SEA	
	RANK SPECIALITY 1 HILTON **** SWIMMING POOL 2 PACIFIC **** SEA FOOD 3 RAMADA **** CASINO 4 STUMP INN * POKER SCHOOL
R3 0412 2N 1M (Reserve, hotel no. 3, 1 male, 2 nights, from 4th December)	
	3 RAMADA FROM 0412 2 NIGHTS 1 MALE RESERVED OK

Fig. 67 *'Menu' selection of options*

other business). So that we can print itineraries and tickets,
we should like a printer as well as a television-screen like
display ('Cathode Ray Tube' or CRT, which is generally
much faster than a device which produces printed output,
'hard copy').

We need either device to respond well inside seven seconds
—the threshold of irritation, after which both customer and
clerk will lose patience. If there is a good reason for delay—
for example, the need for the distant computer to retrieve
some infrequently used information—, the system should be
designed to display a suitable 'hang on' indicator, rather
than appear to go to sleep. Human beings do the same: they
say 'Er . . .'. Some otherwise excellent systems fail to take
account of this simple psychological requirement.

The mini-computer can check the format of the entries
made by the clerks (for example, dates with months outside
the range 01 to 12) and thus save the central computer's time.
It can compress messages for transmission, and check

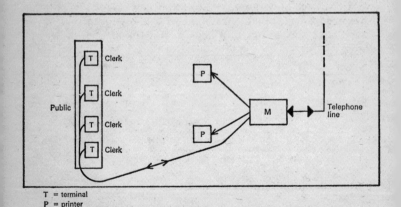

T = terminal
P = printer
M = mini-computer

Fig. 68 *Airline sales office*

incoming messages for transmission errors. If the telephone line fails, the mini-computer can queue up reservations for a while, perhaps on a miniature tape or disc, until the line is restored, although during this time the clerks will have to make do with timetables and seat availability lists on paper or microfilm form. (Such an arrangement is termed a 'fall-back' mode: one which allows us to continue the service to customers, although at a 'degraded' level. When the full service is restored, the transactions done in 'fall-back' mode have to be communicated to the central computer, and this too requires a special procedure: 'recovery'.)

Using the box in Fig. 68 as a 'black box' we can draw a suitable network: the most obvious is a 'star'.

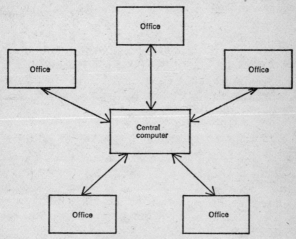

Fig. 69 *Star network*

In practice other networks are also used, for example, 'multi drop' connections, in which one office receives messages *via* one or more other offices: i.e. one line is used by several terminals.

We have seen, in Chapter 2, how terminals can be connected to a central computer and can send and receive messages, either at the bidding of the central computer (which then 'polls' them) or on their own initiative (sending 'interrupts' to the central computer, demanding an opportunity to send a message or to receive one). Similar techniques apply here.

The central computer will look much like those employed on slower-response systems, and may indeed be of the same type. However, it must be capable of the following functions:

(a) Ability to survive failures in component parts. This means that components are duplicated and can be switched in as needed. It also means that, even if a component failed while in the middle of a calculation (i.e. the central processor) or a tape or disc transfer, the information loss is repairable. It means lastly that the central processor can detect malfunctions, usually by a system of 'interrupts' like those which arise when tape or disc transfers are completed, but in this case indicating trouble. For example, if the electricity supply fails, the computer can run on for a few milliseconds, during which time it abandons its current processing and switches in batteries and/or a standby generator.

(b) A special operating system, which allows the same section of program to be in use for several different transactions at the same time. Let us consider a little subroutine for testing whether a flight is full up or not. It has to check a flight number like ABC 336 and a date 0612.

First of all it may need to look up an index to find where, somewhere on disc, the actual flight record is held. Then it uses this to read the record. Now there may be very many clerks enquiring about seat availability on many different flights. The first enquiry causes our little subroutine to start, but soon it is halted, waiting for the disc drive to complete its seek and read. Must all other enquiries wait as well? The index they want may be on a different drive, which may be idle at present. It would be a pity not to use the subroutine for them as well. Accordingly, we allow the subroutine to be temporarily abandoned while the record address for ABC 336 is being retrieved: and another enquiry is allowed to use it, starting from the beginning. As a result our little subroutine may be in use by several different enquiries at once. When the disc drive holding one index finishes its reading, the operating system allows the corresponding enquiry to resume its use of the subroutine—now proceeding to read the record itself, when, once again, there will be a hold-up while a disc drive gets the information requested. You may think of the central processor as full of subroutines, and of transactions in process: the operating system intervenes each time an interrupt occurs, and allows a halted transaction to resume using a subroutine. Each transaction accordingly has its own *routeing block* of information in memory which specifies which subroutines it must use to be completed, and how far it has got. A reasonable analogy would be a big hospital, where patients may be given a routeing card detailing the departments they should visit: perhaps half a dozen are at the X-ray examination department at various stages. When a machine becomes free, the administrator selects a patient, who resumes his passage through the department until, after all X-ray photographs have been taken, he passes on to the next department.

Sometimes someone is unlucky and keeps missing opportunities to proceed. In this case a human patient can complain, but a transaction can only be noticed by the operating system as meriting a little queue-jumping, because the time the transaction first arrived is written at the front of its routeing block and is obviously a long time ago—maybe five seconds!

(c) The central processor needs a 'clock' which it can consult with a suitable computer instruction, and also use like an egg-timer to interrupt itself at a predetermined time in the future.

This is useful to the operating system as a means of detecting trouble. For example, if it reaches an instruction which causes the central processor to send a message over the telephone lines to a terminal in Hong Kong, within two or three seconds it will expect to be interrupted by a message back composed by the minicomputer in Hong Kong to say the message has arrived. In this situation, no news is bad news, so the operating system will set the 'egg-timer' to interrupt whatever instructions which are being obeyed in three seconds' time—probably dealing with some quite unrelated terminal—and to transfer control to part of the operating system which will take suitable action. This may be another attempt at transmitting the message, or eventually a warning to the communications (human or computer) switching system to test the line and try a different routeing. If the message arrives on time, this safety precaution can be cancelled.

There are other situations in which the operating system can start something and must intervene if it does not end properly. Consider the following snatch of program, written when the programmer had a hangover, perhaps (see Fig. 70).

We can see that this program might work satisfactorily until one day a strict Jewish passenger who was also a vegetarian arrived. Then the program would go round procedures MEALS and SPECIAL indefinitely. (Try it out.) In a simple computer system the operator would notice that the computer had stopped reading

```
MEALS.
        IF VEGETARIAN PERFORM VEGA-MEAL.
        IF KOSHER PERFORM KOSHER-MEAL.
        IF VEGETARIAN AND KOSHER GO TO SPECIAL.
        GO TO HOTEL-BOOKING.
                    .
                    .
                    .
                    .
                    .
SPECIAL.
        IF VEGETARIAN OR KOSHER GO TO MEALS.
                    .
                    .
                    .
                    .
```

Fig. 70 *A dangerous piece of program* *(COBOL)*

cards or printing lines and was just going round and round instructions in the central processor's memory, and would stop the job and call the programmer to investigate. But in a multi-thread system (the term used for a computer system in which many transactions are in process at the same time using the same subroutines where necessary) the computer will just keep going, and only this unfortunate passenger's transaction will be stuck. Somewhere a reservations clerk will be banging his terminal and wondering why he gets no answer.

Accordingly when the operating system allowed MEALS to start work on this passenger's requirements, it set a time limit of perhaps half a second for calculations to be done, and if this was exceeded without any messages emerging, the operating system fears the worst and cancels the transaction with suitable calls for attention from the systems and programming support team.

A similar situation can arise when two subroutines are active and are competing for the same records from disc—say a passenger and an airport record. Under certain circumstances they can each be waiting for the other, like two polite people at a door. This is termed 'the Deadly Embrace', and there are techniques for programmers to use which avoid the problem, if it is foreseen. But if they inadvertently forget to use these techniques, the 'egg-timer' reminder to the operating system traps the error. (The term 'watch-dog timer' is in fact used rather than 'egg-timer'!)

You may note that the operating system may have to keep track of a large number of times in the future at which it expects something to have happened. It does not need this number of timers though: it will keep a list of times in memory, with references to the corresponding events, and the timer will be set to interrupt (go 'ping!') at the due time of the *earliest* such event. When this happens, the timer will be reset to cover the next event. Whenever an event happens before its latest time (as should happen normally) the associated entry in the list is removed.

(d) So that information will not be lost if trouble occurs, the operating system will often take copies of all messages on to tape or disc, and go through the main files copying the latest state of records in a cyclical fashion. If the system 'crashes', these copies can be used in the recovery stage, when information lost or destroyed can be re-created. Note that 'crashes' of this kind are more often due to software, i.e. programmer error in the operating system, or in application programs (like Fig. 68) than to electronic component or mechanical failures. For this reason, it is not adequate to try to achieve security by 'duplexing' computers, i.e. having two systems running in parallel, each cross-checking the other.

You may see from the features needed by a large-scale

rapid-response system that the equipment, operating system, and applications programs are liable to be big, complex, and expensive.

We have used the term 'rapid-response' for the systems described in this chapter. '*Real-time*' is another common term, which was originally derived from the early days of simulation, when, after scientists had managed to get a computer to calculate successive positions of a missile as quickly as the missile would go through them when actually fired, the simulation was called 'real-time'. In practice they soon achieved better than real-time, as in the star model described earlier. Nowadays 'real-time' is applied not to scientific simulations but mainly to commercial and industrial rapid-response systems.

One could perhaps say that *a real-time system is one in which the computer part of the system makes its contribution sufficiently quickly for the human part to be able to wait for it without significant idle time, and without damage to the objectives of the system* (e.g. through customer irritation, or out of date information losing opportunities for more revenue or less cost).

Because real-time systems are rather specialised, 'packages' usually apply to particular computers and industries. The IBM 'PARS' (Passenger Air Reservations System) was developed for the IBM/360 and was modified by IBM, with BOAC, as *I*PARS (*I*nternational PARS). In 1968 allegations were made by BOAC that this expensive investment had been pirated and offered for sale outside the airline: this was one of the first cases in which computer packages were involved in the same disputes which have been long familiar in the fields of patents and copyright.

Holiday firms are catered for by special packages such as Teltour, marketed by a German mail order and store chain, Quelle (the reason why such an organisation should be interested in rapid-response systems will become clear in a later section), and Court Line and Clarksons developed their own. Recently there has been a change in the air travel business which *flexible* reservations systems can cope with: in particular, prices, demand, availability of aircraft pilots and maintenance men, are changeable and a system is needed which can keep revenue up in these difficult times by reacting quickly to such changes. One alternative is, however, to bypass the whole idea of reservations by letting passengers walk on, rather like a bus service. This idea was pioneered by Eastern Airlines in the USA to use up surplus aircraft capacity, but it appeals to the last-minute traveller. The economics of such a scheme can be validated by computer studies, but as might be expected reservations staff may turn against the idea as threatening their jobs. Recent developments include the idea of the traveller identifying himself with a credit card and booking himself through a special terminal at which he indicates his destination: a 'do it yourself' rapid-response system.

Banking

If A gives B a cheque, B pays the cheque into his own account. The bank must allow him the use of this money as soon as possible. But equally the bank wishes to deduct the amount of the cheque from A's account so that it can detect any attempt by A to overdraw. There is thus an incentive to apply the cheque to *both* accounts as quickly as possible. Secondly, bank clerks have become well paid. Thirdly, bank transactions have increased.

Cheque clearing is a medium- to rapid-response system in which the physical document is handled and read as far as possible automatically: each bank's system adds the value of incoming cheques to its own accounts, then separates them according to the payer's bank and transmits them to the other banks and to itself. When each bank has received the cheques drawn on its own accounts, its system then *deducts* the value of these cheques from them. Incidentally GIRO works the other way: if you pay someone, your account is reduced before theirs is increased. This gives GIRO cash in hand on which interest can be earned with the result that charges to customers can be little or none, unless they borrow money (a service just being introduced at the time of writing).

At one time the cheques had to be physically sorted and eventually returned to the drawer, but now most of the information is transmitted by magnetic tape, and the actual documents microfiled for storage. Customers are given more information on the statements but are not given the original cheques back.

An alternative to cheques, for regular payments like mortgage interest, is the direct debit: *no* paper documents are involved. Your computer account record has information stored in it which automatically deducts the amount, and a corresponding amount is credited to the Abbey National or other building society.

After the *clearing* application, banks are turning increasingly to computers to assist in their other activities. An obvious requirement is for the customer and the bank to be able to know the state of the customer's account, and it should show recent activity. Now that customers' accounts are on a central computer system in each large bank, it is no longer possible for the manager in a local branch to walk over to a ledger and look up Mr. Smith's account. One possibility is to arrange for the central computer to produce lists of accounts every night and to have these posted to each branch. This is feasible if microfilm or microfiche is used, as in the system employed by the Standard Bank: in this case an NCR device is used which gives 270 pages of output on a single microfiche. The branch requires a special viewer to read its contents. See Fig. 53.

Alternatively one could have terminals in branches which are connected to the central computer by telephone line, and all customer accounts kept on disc files so that they can be retrieved in any order. This is an expensive solution. For this reason computer manufacturers now offer terminals which can be installed in branches and can either work *on-line*, i.e. continuously in contact with the central computer, or *off-line*, i.e. disconnected, but being loaded with the latest data by telephone line or magnetic tape/disc periodically, and having sufficient power to help in the running of the branch: foreign exchange calculations, interest and charges payable, statistics, balancing the books, etc. Two such systems are the IBM 3600 Finance Communication System and Burroughs' branch control computer. Both employ terminals at counter positions within the branch, and can communicate with a central computer.

At the end of the section on airline reservation systems, it was mentioned that there are now experiments in letting the passenger enquire, reserve a seat, and buy tickets without the intervention of a clerk. Now a common reason why an individual needs to go to a *bank* counter is to get cash. This process is in course of becoming automatic, through the use of *cash dispensers* which provide notes when the customer inserts a special identity card in the machine and presses control buttons. The firm of Chubb, well-known for safes and security equipment, make such a dispenser, and operation is controlled and checked by a *mini-computer* made by General Automation. There is clearly no technical reason why many other bank transactions could not be made automatic too, such as authorising standing orders, enquiring about one's account, obtaining foreign currency, etc. Barclays bank introduced NCR 770 'auto-tellers' in two Oxford branches in 1975, initially working 'off-line' for dispensing cash, then connected to a computer ('on-line') which can check the state of the customer's account before releasing the money. This is the pilot operation for a self-service system in which customers can pay money in as well as draw money out. Earlier we described credit cards accounting. Developments in this field seem to indicate that the days of the familiar imprinter are numbered: shopkeepers may have an electronic card reader which will record the transaction on a small magnetic cassette tape, for example, which can be posted back to the credit card company or transmitted over a telephone line. One suggestion is that the card itself could have a small memory (like a magnetic stripe) which gives the current balance and credit limit: the electronic card reader could check the limit and update (bring up to date by including the latest purchase) the balance. Such a system would reduce the time a transaction is in 'limbo' and enable the shopkeeper to get his remittance from the credit card company faster.

Small is beautiful?

We shall notice how often systems now include small computers right at the scene of a transaction. Petrol pumps may have such a *microprocessor* to control octane mixtures, flow rates, acceptance of notes or credit cards, etc. There is even talk of an 'intelligent spanner' which can adjust its jaws and torque loading through an inbuilt computer. (Mercedes Benz already employ small electronic 'computers' to adjust fuel, air, ignition, etc. to give test performance under all conditions, although these are special purpose devices not quite like the programmable computers covered by this book.) Microprocessors are composed of several thousand components on one or two semiconductor chips, no bigger than a square of chocolate, and cost only £10 in quantity. At one time computer experts wondered whether the costs of data transmission would go down so fast that we should end up with a few very big rapid-response computers connected to simple terminals. What is actually happening is that the costs of miniature central processors, including memory, have fallen much faster. As a result the most economic solution is now generally a *hierarchy* of computers, with cheap *micro*-processors built into cash registers, petrol pumps, etc. which can get information from, and pass the results of transactions to, local *mini*-computers which in turn communicate over *telephone* lines to a central *medium* computer which need not have an exceptionally rapid response. The very large computer complex is thus avoided, and since the bulk of transactions is handled locally, the capacity and cost of telephone lines are reduced.

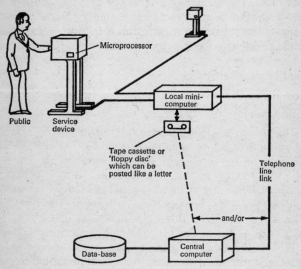

Fig. 71 *Three-level rapid response system, economising on central computer and telephone line charges*

We can see, from the way those most conservative institutions, banks, are moving, that the modern systems analyst must be aware of new kinds of computer which are a cross between the big 'number crunchers' he worked on in the 60's, and pocket calculators. Mammals have now evolved among the dinosaurs! One may wonder why this has happened in spite of what is called 'Grosch's Law', after

Dr. Herb Grosch, who postulated that due to the beneficial effects of scale, if you pay twice as much for a computer you can expect to get four times the power. This is true enough in terms of numbers of multiplications per second, but experience has shown that big computer *installations* soak up money, in support staff particularly, and since the system must be very reliable (because the local parts of the system cannot run at all if the centre breaks down) we may have to duplicate or triplicate it. In the hierarchical system, if the central computer fails for an hour, nobody need notice.

Point of sale systems

Most commercial transactions happen in shops. Their value is, on average, low compared to the sale of an airliner, or an airline ticket. Nevertheless, shop assistants cost wages, and shoplifting, under- or over-charging, running out of stock, and having stock rot on the shelves, are expensive.

As one might expect, National Cash Registers pioneered the field and computers are now definitely involved at the point of sale (POS). Glattzentrum, a big shopping centre near Zurich, has 48 checkout terminals connected to an NCR 726.

Point of sale equipment can cover:

(a) Automatic recognition of the product bought (by some machine-readable code on it).
(b) Pricing of product and addition to bill. VAT or other sales tax.
(c) Counting down stock of this product and warning when a low level has been reached, or when the product is being sold *too* slowly.
(d) Checking and accepting coins, notes, credit card cheque, or customer account.
(e) Control of till balance, and computing and dispensing change and trading stamps.

(f) Salesman's or saleswoman's commission if appropriate.

(g) Tallying transactions and printing receipts.

No doubt these developments are helped by three unpleasant trends: constantly changing prices and taxes, inability of sales staff to do arithmetic, and dishonest customers.

Information retrieval systems

Some rapid-response systems are used to back up people who need to find things out: research scientists interested in previous work in a particular field, or police looking for an individual with certain physical characteristics. Traditionally a reference *book* has been used in the past, but its snag is that it is expensive and difficult to keep up to date. The author is a private pilot, and when planning a flight makes reference to a manual called the *Air Pilot*, without doubt one of the worst organised reference books one could imagine. (It is interesting to note that this criticism will, unfortunately, be resented by nobody, since the *Air Pilot* is the result of the deliberations of many committees at national and international levels.)

In contrast, a telephone directory, because reference is made always by one simple key—name—is easy and quick to use, but some extreme types of enquiry are very difficult to answer without a complete scan of the material, for example:

> *Enquiry 1*
> Names of persons convicted of burglary, with black hair, or bald: 30 to 50 years old: Scottish.

It can, however, be done, at some cost in complication. Consider a simple list of people known to the police (Fig. 72).

We could arrange for each of these malefactors to have his or her record on magnetic tape, and collect up a whole list

Name		Date of birth	Convictions Burglary Murder ...		(Other information)
ADAM, ABOU BEN	M	1923	✓		
ARAM, EUGENE	M	1940		✓	

Fig. 72 *List of malefactors*

of enquiries 1, 2 . . . Every night the computer will read all the enquiries, and then the entire file, testing each record in turn to see if it is an answer to *any* enquiry. The time taken to do this will depend much more on the number of male-factors than the number of enquiries, and so to keep down computer running time we would like to run the job *in*-frequently and so provide a *slow* response time (on average equal to half the interval between runs):

There is a mistake in Fig. 73. Try to discover what it is and check the answer in Appendix 8.

In practice we would probably not print out matching malefactors straight away, but put their details on a *work* file on disc or tape, and *sort* them by enquiry, so that each enquirer does not have to wade through every other en-quirer's report.

Consider now the situation where a police car is following a vehicle which behaves suspiciously. The police use their car radio to call up an operator sitting at a computer terminal: 'Anything bad known about the owner of **GMO 824K**?' The tape system above would be to slow.

But if there is a file of malefactors on a *disc* file, with an index by vehicle also on disc, the operator can key in

GMO 824K

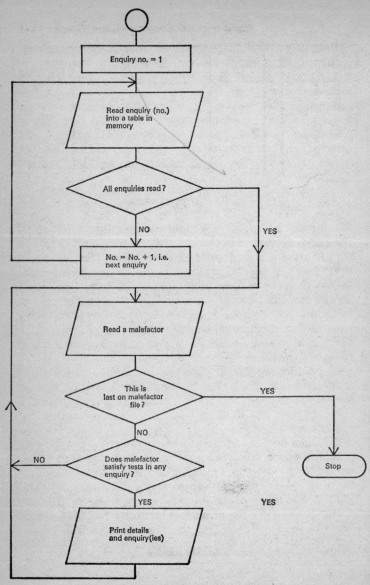

Fig. 73 *Logic diagrams for enquiries*

at the terminal and the program can consult the index, maybe structured at two levels: see Fig 74.

The computer will need to obey at least three disc file seeks and reads to get the information, which the operator can then relay to the car. The driver can then decide whether it might be fruitful to pursue GMO 824K further. It is possible that the car might be equipped with a transmitter directly connected by radio to the computer so that the police officer can key in the registration number, and get

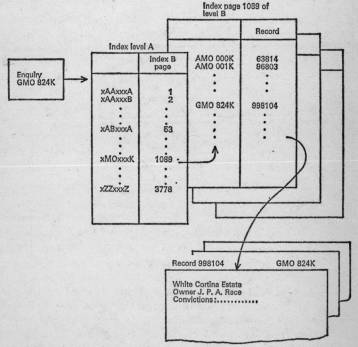

Fig. 74 *Rapid response enquiry system: levels of indexing (the information is in practice held on discs as in Fig. 30)*

back the details by a computer-generated voice, or printer, in the car:

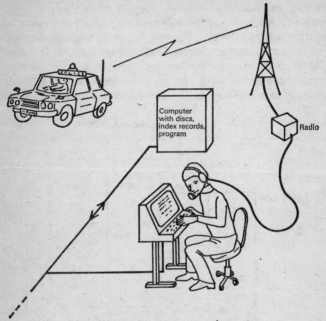

Fig. 75 *Rapid response enquiry system*

To be used efficiently the computer program must be designed to handle several enquiries at once, i.e. have the requirements noted for airline systems.

At present there are two computer systems in the UK which are relevant to this discussion: the centralised licensing system at Swansea, which is now operating after some delays due to the enormous problem of setting up the data-files from the previously decentralised authorities, and the police system based on Burroughs computers at Hendon. Criminologists have noted that convictions for driving offences are strongly correlated with general criminality, and cars are often involved in crime directly. Accordingly we can expect these two systems—the Swansea one basically a medium-response administrative system and the Hendon one, a rapid-response criminal data interrogation system—to become eventually integrated, unless for other reasons this is felt not to be in the public interest. As things are, if a policeman asks to see your licence, the Swansea computer tells him if you have been convicted because it will have written this on the licence. But in the future the policemen on your tail may know what's on your licence before he stops you.

Now, if we add together the requirements of the earlier example—'Enquiry 1'—and the 'GMO 824K' example, we are asking the computer to respond rapidly to *compound* questions like:

'Tell me if we have anything on the driver of a white Cortina Estate, with registration letters GMO or CMO but rest not known: male driver, looks about 45.'

Human beings are remarkably good at retrieving information from such partial clues (provided the total number of entries is reasonably small, i.e. less than 10 000 or so), but computer systems are surprisingly clumsy. What can be done is to provide methods for retrieving according to any one of several keys, so that the computer can find records for all drivers of a given age, or with cars of a particular colour. The program can determine which test is most definite and likely to produce the smallest number of matching records, and then go through these, applying the other tests to eliminate more of them.

Such a procedure will entail many more disc accesses, than the single-key approach, and the large amount of cross-referencing will mean that whenever a new record is added to the files, many linkages to other related records will need to be set up, and this will also involve several disc reads and writes.

6

Trends: Data-Bases, CAD, Minis and Micros, Ultra-fast Systems, Systems in the Home

In the last chapter we touched on systems like the 'malefactor search', which require a computer to retrieve information in answer to a question posed by an enquirer in the form of retrieval keys and selection rules. We will now discuss how this ability can be achieved, and later on in the chapter, cover a number of other significant developments in computing today: computer-aided-design (CAD), and the new generation of small 'mini' and 'micro' computers which are cheap enough to be built into domestic appliances.

Theoretical work has led to the idea of the 'data-base', which is a way of looking at files of information on a computer as *models* of things and their properties and relationships, in the real world: for example, a family of husband and wife, two children, might be represented by a set of disc records linked by 'pointers' or numbers which indicate where in the disc file a related record is held (see Fig. 76(a)). The records for each member of the family might be as shown in Fig. 76(b).

We must have a master-record in the system giving the *first* record in each chain. This technique enables us to traverse records in a file without having an index. For example, suppose we want to list all *daughters* with both parents on file, i.e. presumably alive. We could do this by the logic shown in Fig. 77.

The software, i.e. 'Operating System' level programs need-

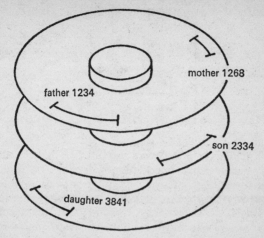

Fig. 76(a) *A family on disc. The numbers represent the record address, i.e. what the program needs, to issue seeks and reads to find the corresponding record.*

ed to set up a data base is elaborate, but when installed, allows the systems analyst and programmer great freedom: in an application program they can now write statements such as

> CALL GET—ENQUIRY;
> CALL RETRIEVE (ENQUIRY.KEY);

GET—ENQUIRY is a sub-routine which arranges for a terminal to transmit a set of identifiers (KEY) defining the information required, and RETRIEVE does the necessary searching of indexes or chained records until the right record or records are found. This is much neater than the analyst and programmer having to design the complicated matching business themselves—in this case, much more involved than that described in Fig. 29 ('simple' magnetic tape processing). But although it looks neat, the analyst must remember that the single statement starts the central

Record address	Data			Pointers to other records					
	name	sex	etc.	Eldest child	Sibling	Same sex	Spouse	Parent	etc.
Father's 1234	JOHN	M	.....	2334	—	2334	1268	—	
Mother's 1268	MARY	F	.....	2334	—	3841	1234	—	
Son's 2334	FRED	M	.....	—	3841	9638*	—	1234	
Daughter's 3841	ANNE	F	.....	—	2334	8774*	—	1234	

* Addresses of records of unrelated people of same sex

Fig. 76(b) *Records chained by 'pointers'*

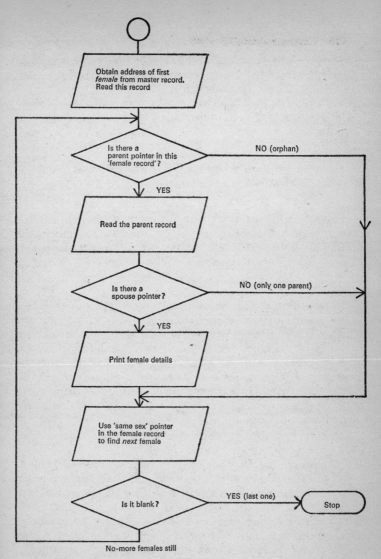

Fig. 77 *Processing a data-base: following a chain of linked records*

processor and disc files off on a considerable processing task, and one which will be extremely expensive if the file organisation has been badly chosen.

In the author's CHASER system, a manager can retrieve information at a terminal using a simple 'mnemonic language', e.g.

SEL
ANY [order-item number between 1000 and 1500]
AND [overdue for delivery]
END

produces a list, in order-item sequence, of certain overdue order-items. The program which analyses the mnemonic commands like SEL, etc. written in 'CHASER' language, uses in turn sub-routines, e.g.

CALL KBX (I, 1, NUM)

which in this case stores an order item number in an index. But subroutine KBX itself is quite involved, because the index entry to be set up may be on a disc file or in central processor memory, and if the former, the appropriate section of index must be located and read into memory by KBX. So simple requests by user and application programmer are expanded to achieve the desired result. In the early development of CHASER, it was found that excessive amounts of computer time were used in certain types of retrieval, and the data-base was re-designed, cutting down processing costs by a factor of about five.

The moral of all this is that we can *in principle* provide simple, logical methods for solving any data retrieval problem, but that if rapid-response *and* a complex structured file are involved, it will cost a great deal of money. The alert systems analyst may be able to redefine the requirements, or find out which are the *commonest* modes of use, and so keep costs down. If rapid response and complexity are both essential, the benefits of the system had better be considerable.

There are many types of data-base software available: 'Informatics Mark IV' is a medium-response enquiry processing program (which can also add, delete and change records) on the lines of Fig. 72 (list of malefactors). ICL's FIND does a similar job.

Hierarchically ordered data bases for faster-response systems are covered by software such as IBM IMS, or RAMIS. Chained systems, which can cut across hierarchical structures, can be set up using IDS (Integrated Data Storage) on Honeywell/GE computers. There is even a special language called LISP for dealing with complicated chained data structures (in central processor memory, not on tape or disc, which rather limits the volumes it can handle).

The COBOL language, however, can be extended to handle data stored according to the data-base philosophy instead of the more orthodox files accessed by the READ and WRITE statements you will remember from the example in Fig. 10. Recommendations on the 'grammar' and 'syntax' of these extensions have been published by CODASYL, the committee responsible for COBOL (rather as L'Académie Française is responsible for French!). Similarly PL/1 can handle data-bases through IBM-supported variants of this language.

The design of data-base software is a challenging area of computer science, since flexibility, efficiency and rapid-response are difficult to achieve together. Professor Stocker of Essex University has developed the idea of data-base software which actually notes which records and retrieval keys are used most frequently, and alters the structure of the files to improve performance accordingly, on the assumption that there will not be a sudden swing to examine other records or use other keys.

Human beings solve crosswords, or recognise people, using several clues simultaneously rather like turning many searchlights simultaneously on to an area of ground, and so illuminating a small area in which the answer is to be found. Computers at present can 'shine' but one 'searchlight', and plod along the much bigger area illumined by it to find the answer. However, our ability is not due to some spiritual or mystic property of mind, and recent work on *parallel processing* and *associative memory* leads us to expect that computers will perform better in this regard in the future.

Computer-aided design ('CAD')

Consider an engineer designing an instrument for the cockpit of an aircraft. He has to make sure that:

it can fit in the panel
it can be seen by the pilot
it responds (e.g. by needle deflection) to electrical or mechanical signals, according to the specifications
it can be made easily, and preferably out of components already available.

Traditionally he can attack the first two problems by drawings and by mock-ups. Even so it is not unknown to find that under some circumstances an instrument is obscured, by a rather tall co-pilot's head when he is reaching for a switch, for example. However, it is possible to describe the cockpit and its inhabitants, in three-dimensional space, and to define the possible motions of those parts of it that can move: to give a computer this description, and to run a program which can analyse the space for situations which we want to avoid. It can also display these situations by drawing them on a graph plotter, e.g. Fig. 78.

The next problem is to design the instrument itself. Let us suppose it is to work electronically. We can draw a circuit diagram showing the transistors, capacitors, resistors, etc. We now wish to check that the circuit responds accurately to a range of input voltages with the correct output signals, even when the instrument is subjected to various combi-

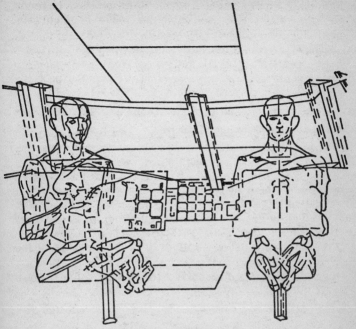

Fig. 78 *Computer-produced picture of cockpit*
(From Fetter, paper in Eurocomp conference 1974)

nations of heat, overload, power supply variations, etc. Once again, we may use a computer, in this instance to draw, on a television-tube-like display screen, a picture of the circuit and to show the results under the range of circumstances we have defined. We may decide to alter the circuit connections or the value of a component, i.e. a larger capacitor, and may do this by means of a 'light pen' placed against the screen (see Fig. 79).

The 'light pen' appears to draw lines on the screen, although in fact it works in a different and rather interesting way. The computer itself draws a small cross or other symbol on the screen, and keeps doing this many times a second by sending commands from the central processor to the television tube to produce the result in Fig. 80. The commands are:

—deflect the electron beam 50 units of .01 to the right while modulating it to brighten the screen,
—deflect it 25 units up and 25 units left *without* brightening the screen,
—deflect it 50 units down while brightening the screen.

Now the light pen has a small photo-sensitive cell at its tip, which will detect brightness on the screen where it rests, and the central processor can test this, at a point in the program when the electron beam has been directed to the centre of the cross. If the light pen responds 'Yes—light detected', it is thus positioned on the centre of the cross. If we move it away from the centre of the cross, the program may execute an instruction such as IF(.NOT.BRIGHT) CALL FINDPEN and a sub-routine FINDPEN will rapidly move the electron beam to various points in the area of the position where the pen was last known to be, and brighten each

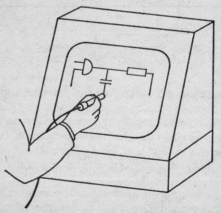

Fig. 79 *Interactive graphics*

point in turn: if at one of these points it finds the condition BRIGHT it will assume that it has found the new position of the pen. If the human operator is drawing a line (which he may indicate by a switch of some kind) the program will cause the electron beam to brighten up the line connecting its old and new positions—in fact it can 'straighten out' a shaky line drawn freehand by the operator.

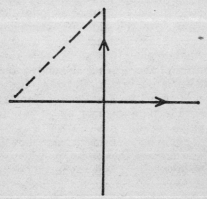

Fig. 80 *Drawing a cross on a visual display*

In a similar way lines can be erased, and whole sub-assemblies of lines (e.g. representing the symbol for a transistor or a cogwheel) can be moved bodily about the screen by the operator. One may say, this is rather an expensive substitute for a pencil and paper! But the point is that once the current circuit diagram is defined to the computer, its calculating power can be applied to checking, analysing, revising, and tidying up the human being's ideas. We have a perfect combination of human inventiveness backed up by electronic accuracy and speed.

We come to the last aspect of the problem—how do we actually manufacture the instrument? Ideally we shall try to make it out of standard components, and again the screen can be used to show components which have previously been designed and built—like a standard dial or housing—and the designer can call for these by part number or after getting the computer to give him a list of all dials, or housings, with brief details, from which he selects the one he thinks will be most appropriate. He can then build up a picture on the screen of the completed instrument, and when satisfied, can get the image reproduced in a more permanent form by a graph plotter or by recording the image optically. This then forms a specification for assembling the instrument. If an item has to be made, like a turned spindle, it is possible for the computer to produce a tape, from the current definition it has of the item's shape and layout, which can then be loaded on to a numerically controlled machine tool which will then cut it out. The Decca radar dish at London Airport was made in this manner, and it was unnecessary to produce a physical prototype.

This use of computers is being promoted by the Computer Aided Design Centre at Cambridge, in fields as dissimilar as the design of shoes and of highway junctions. In the case of an integrated electronic circuit, the computer-produced layout can be photographically reduced down to postage-stamp size, and then used as a mask to etch the required connections and electronic components on to a wafer of semiconductor. In this way all the stages from the definition of an electronic function required, such as a pulse generator giving a square wave of 10 megaherz (10 million a second), right through to the tiny sugar-cube-sized products emerging from the machine which embeds them in plastic, can be automated.

Similarly, the printed circuit boards on to which these components will be soldered can be produced 'untouched by human hand' from a computer-generated layout. REDAC Software, part of the RACAL Electronics Group, specialise in the use of computers for designing electronic components and circuits in this way.

Minis and micros

Like skirts, computers started coming in abbreviated versions in recent years, though unlike skirts, the mini/micro fashion in computers seems here to stay.

Minicomputers became popular first with a small, reliable, simple computer called the PDP8 made by the US Digital Equipment Corporation, designed to be used *outside* the computer department: built into other machines for monitoring and controlling plant, surveying the sea-bed and so on. It could be used for the local communications control job described in the last chapter (see Fig. 68). The programs were written in a language close to that of the machine's own language. Other firms like Ferranti were, at this time, producing digital computers for aircraft navigation and fire-control, and these small, reliable machines found their way into a wider market.

The relatively low cost of a mini produced in bulk meant that in many industrial processes it was cheaper to incorporate a computer in the control and monitoring system than to design special electrical, electronic, or mechanical systems. Moreover the computer can be re-programmed more easily than a fixed-control system can be physically modified. This area of work is termed *process control*.

Suppose we have a chemical plant with two chemicals flowing into a reactor: they are to enter at given temperatures within given margins of error, and the reactor itself is to be held within a third temperature range. Refrigeration and heating controls must be adjusted, levels checked, etc. (see Fig. 81).

The relationships between the positions of cocks C_1, C_2 and C_3, the levels in the tanks L_1, L_2 and L_3, the temperatures T_1, T_2 and T_3, and the heating/cooling exchangers H_1, H_2 and H_3 will be complicated but expressible as mathematical formulae.

We can imagine wires coming *from* the Ls and Ts, bringing

information *into* the computer, and wires going *to* the Cs and Hs *from* the computer, causing them to vary flows and heating/cooling inputs so as to bring the Ls and Ts into the desired range and keep them there.

There are three reasons for using a computer rather than a human being. Firstly, the computer is cheaper, especially when employed 24 hours a day, seven days a week. Secondly, the computer can respond faster. Suppose the reactor in the above example can process 100 gallons an hour at 200°C and 150 gallons an hour if run at 240°C. However, it must not be

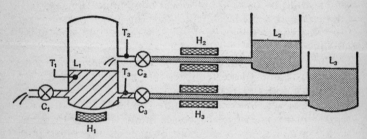

Fig. 81 *An industrial process, suitable for computer control*

allowed to reach 250°C, since this would cause an explosion. By the nature of the process, at 240°C the reaction can 'run away' if not cooled within a few seconds of it starting to get hotter. A human controller could well fail to turn on the cooling fast enough. Hence we might have to run it at 200°C at which level there might be a minute's safety margin, but at the cost of running at a third of the potential capacity. The use of a computer avoids this loss and may save its own cost many times over in its first year of operation. In process control too, therefore, the economics of using computers is bound up with *response time*. Thirdly, a computer is more reliable.

Process control in chemical plants, refineries, air-conditioning for large buildings, and so on has been accelerated by the availability of the 'minicomputer', the cost of which is kept down by

(a) moderate speed
(b) omission of circuitry to do the more sophisticated commercial and scientific data manipulations
(c) small physical size with reduced installation costs
(d) large production runs
(e) modest operating systems, compilers, and 'packages'
(f) the user himself designing the software for the job

Many were originally developed by control and instrument companies like Honeywell and Hewlett-Packard. Yet the second generation of 'minicomputers' has now started to invade the preserve of the traditional big computers, with the addition of tapes and discs, line printers, COBOL compilers, etc.

In the last year or two, a new phenomenon has appeared—*the microprocessor*. This device is a small integrated circuit on a 'chip', about the size of a sugar cube, designed and manufactured with computer help as described earlier. It was introduced as a natural step in the movement to putting more and more components—resistors, capacitors, transistors—on to a single chip, by electronic component manufacturers like Texas Instruments, Intel, RCA. Each chip can perform the function of a simple central processor, i.e. obey a series of instructions, fetch and send data from and to a memory, test for interrupts and so on, but usually relatively slowly, e.g. taking a hundred millionths rather than one millionth of a second to add two numbers, and these numbers have to be of limited size. Nevertheless, the miniature programs which control the operation (stored on special Read Only Memory or ROM, or Programmable Read Only Memory (PROM) which can be reloaded with a different program by a special process) can carry out quite complicated operations on bigger numbers by tackling them a piece at a time. These are the devices at the heart of a hand-held calculator.

Another use for microprocessors is in managing a 'memory', i.e. decoding demands for data from another (bigger scale) central processor, and interrogating the core storage, checking for errors, etc. A firm of mini-computer manufacturers, General Automation, use them incorporated in the leads from their central processor to the peripheral devices like Teletype terminals—they call these leads 'intelligent cables'!

To some extent one might think that microprocessors are only a minor technical innovation for convenience and flexibility, simply substituting a microprogram stored in a ROM plus a little processor to execute it, for a specially designed circuit with discrete components. Certainly for the systems analyst, a business computer which uses microprocessors behaves much like one built from conventional circuits: it may perhaps be easier for the engineers to modify to carry out special new functions, perhaps, but otherwise there is no external difference.

But there are two ways in which microprocessors may make a big impact. One is in the field of process control at the small end of the range: instead of mini-computer controlled chemical plants, we can think of bus engines or petrol pumps or even washing machines controlled *economically* by microprocessors. After all, the electromechanical programmer of a washing machine is a complicated device which is open to competition from an electronic, compact computer costing less than £10 in bulk.

Secondly, the microprocessor may be used in large numbers as a substitute for a single, big processor, to do certain kinds of computation where calculations can proceed in parallel, as in weather forecasting. In essence each microprocessor has access to its own memory for holding the results of intermediate calculations, and also can send and obtain values from other microprocessors. All the microprocessors operate at once, so that 'ripples' of computation travel across an array of them. Professor Dijkstra has mentioned two particular scientific-sounding applications for such assemblages of 'mosquitoes humming in harmony': ultra-fast Fourier transforms, and matrix arithmetic. In case these applications sound rather theoretical, Fourier transforms are close to the heart of the solution to problems in pattern recognition and thus to artificial intelligence, and matrix arithmetic is a mathematical name for what goes on in what an accountant would call the 'extension' of an invoice (multiplying quantities by prices and adding the products) or in the 'explosion' of a proposed production program into piece part requirements. In this book we have mostly dealt with the remarkable capabilities of existing computers, but the author believes that after a period of twenty years in which the original idea of the digital computer was really only refined and developed, we are on the brink of some totally new technological advances.

Ultra-fast response systems

In this book we progressed from slow-response systems to those which can keep up with a human being who is dealing with a customer, or is designing a new machine: responding with assistance in the form of information or analysis in seconds. In this chapter we have mentioned systems which have to match physical processes which need an even faster response than a human being, like a reactor being run close to the edge of 'run-away', or an anti-aircraft missile that must turn almost instantaneously when its target dodges. What faster responses could there be?

One very rapid electronic process with which we are all familiar is the television. The circuitry in our TV operates at speeds in excess of most computers: the information on a screen consists of 625 lines each with a resolution of over

500 picture points each of several tones or colours: the information transfer rate is in the megaherz range, i.e. many million bits (binary digits) per second. If we try to run a TV at less than this speed we shall get unacceptable flickering of the image.

Work is now in hand on computers which can intervene in the production of TV pictures—to improve quality, extract and process symbolic information, generate pictures, and so on. The trend in communications is for the information to be transmitted in a *symbolic* form to save the power and cost of transmitters, and for the local receiver to translate the symbols into understandable sounds or images. For example, the letters printed along the top of the card in Fig. 19 are in the form of a dot pattern in a 7 × 5 rectangle, i.e. needing 35 'bits', i.e. dot/no-dot values. And on this page, the letters are of much better definition, needing a rectangle of more like 200 × 100 each. But the number of *different* possible letters/figures in a punched card is less than 256, which can be represented by only 8 bits. So for transmitting information we save by encoding at the sending station and decoding at the receiving. This is not yet done with TV broadcasting, but there is scope for the transmission of coded symbols which computer-like processors in the TV receiver convert into legible text.

Even the picture itself can be a suitable case for treatment: much of the time pictures change little between successive frames, and within one frame, there are blocks of undifferentiated colour. The transmitter could just send changes, and coded instructions like 'red triangle in position . . . dimensions . . .' instead of spelling it out point by point. The decoding of such instructions is a job for a simple, very high-speed computer.

The ultimate is perhaps a transmitter which just transmits the code designating a particular individual, and his or her orientation, and the receiver generates the required profile or full face on the screen! This may seem exotic, but considerable work has been done on the generation of synthetic scenes by high-speed computers—the scene specified in general terms by an overall controller, but converted into a coloured, moving, perspective view by a computer embedded in the video circuits. Such a system is in use for flight simulators, where the 'specification' of the scene is given by the pseudo-aircraft's current:

> longitude,
> latitude,
> altitude,
> bank,
> pitch,
> azimuth heading,

which six values are converted into a scene showing a horizon (suitably inclined if the aircraft is banking) and a landscape with fields, runways, even hills, buildings and trees.

Computer-based systems in the home

The long-term prospects are that such techniques could lead us to computers as *entertainment* devices linked to TV sets, giving us realistic pictures *under our control*: perhaps we can have a knob by which we can select which characters are to appear at a given juncture! Already we see electronic tennis games available on TV sets, and eventually low cost, high-speed computers may expand these developments in some surprising directions, foreseen by science-fiction writers for many years, but now becoming practical as the cost of electronic circuitry falls, and the cost of almost everything else rises.

It is interesting to count the number of electric motors in one's house. If we include clocks, shavers, pumps, turntables, car heaters, hair driers, etc. the total will probably reach twenty. The small, cheap reliable electric motor installed just where it is needed has given us power in any device in which it is needed: the old Victorian factory system of a single engine driving machines via shafts, belts and pulleys could never have been used to mechanise the home. Similarly we may see microprocessors installed in all those *systems* in the home which have to do with information: TV, telephone, hi-fi, microfilm library (we shall have to give up cutting down trees to store information in), housekeeping accounts, pantry/cooker/deep-freeze stock control and production control (cooking!).

It is unlikely we shall see a huge central computer controlling these devices remotely: partly because, on present showing, industrial action by its operators could paralyse the country almost instantaneously, and partly because running high capacity cables to each house is much more expensive than supplying the processing power on the spot.

For personal communications with the outside world we would use the telephone, whose microprocessor would pass information on to the others (e.g. pass on gas bills to the housekeeping system). Other, bulky communications of more general interest like stock market reports, French courses, or cricket scores would be transmitted by TV, but with signals compressed by the techniques mentioned and only intercepted and replayed by those people who want them.

7

Wider Issues: Ethics, Metaphysics, and What the Reader should do about Computers

In the introductory chapter we argued that computers raise important issues which laymen as well as professionals should think about. Computers give us artificial brain-power just as steam gave us artificial muscle-power: these powers have a profound effect on our social and economic life. Because we can now solve most problems if we really want to, we have to think perhaps for the first time whether in fact we should: what our priorities should be. Again, how can societies like a limited company or a local authority, made up of variously motivated individuals, communicating not only by English but also by tones of voice, and movements of the body, bring into their councils a machine which can make a unique contribution in terms of rapid arithmetic and data retrieval, but which can only be communicated with through languages even more formal than English, let alone through 'body language' or the unspoken hint? The systems analyst becomes a sort of priest to the computer's oracle, translating what he thinks are the requests of his clients into the oracle's terms. He is rarely trained to look more deeply into the clients' requests, and to see that there is often an unspoken element—a need for psychological reassurance, or to express aggression. He would probably resist having to play such a role, since to work with computers means having to think with a profound directness and obviousness. Why, for example, did a computer when faced with:

$$A = B = C$$

always make A equal to 1 or 0 instead of setting it to the value of C: and why was B unchanged? The analyst's mind must work with computer-like simplicity: in this case the computer first asked the question:

What is the value of $(B = C)$, i.e. true or false?

Then it placed this answer, converted to a number (true = 1, false = 0) in A. (This example is from PL/1.)

How can a man who thinks like this appreciate that when the works manager asks for a forecast of sales of product A, he is in fact firing the first round in a political battle with the marketing director? But if the analyst *can* communicate on all these levels, calmly and without cynicism, accepting the limitations of computer nature and human nature (not forgetting his own) he will help his organisation to use its computer and, almost more important, understand its own drives and structure. The reader is referred to Ivor Catt's book *Computer Worship* for a thorough attack on computers and the people who design, sell, program and use them. But similar books could have been written when fire was first used, the wheel invented, or money introduced. It is true we have faults which computer systems can illuminate rather too brightly for comfort, but human beings are nothing if not adaptable when a new discovery holds out promise of making life richer, safer, healthier and more interesting.

One possible consequence of computers—certainly observable in the staff meetings of academic computer scientists! —is a much greater degree of openness in discourse, when people in a group express their attitudes and opinion of others' attitudes with no reticence about ambition, money, sex or religion. Everything is explicit, there is no room for misunderstanding, and if a computer is to be involved in a system for which the group is responsible, its role can be defined clearly because those of the human beings are not partly obscured by decent fig-leaves. But at the time of writing this attitude of mind is not much in evidence at the corporate and governmental levels, and in the author's view, the chances of a computer truly participating in the management of such big enterprises (as distinct from providing support, as in the case of Corporate Planning discussed in Chapter 5), are indeed low.

A more metaphysical issue can be raised: 'can computers think?' This kind of question is not easily answered by describing the actual capabilities of computers: the fact that they can be programmed to play reasonable chess will not persuade those against the proposition, and those for it may argue that being able to add one plus one is a sufficient argument. In fact the question is about what our *attitude* to computers should be. Obviously we should behave differently when faced with a thinking rather than a non-thinking thing. A similar situation applies to the distinction between living and non-living things. Western Europeans disapprove of cruelty to large mammals like horses and dogs: they will however step on cockroaches quite cheerfully. Our behaviour is not really *inconsistent*, since we take each case individually. General arguments justifying our attitudes have never been very popular, and a thorough-going belief in the sanctity of all life (as practised by the strictest Hindus) would lead to a degree of discomfort we would reject. Accordingly we have to consider the question 'can computers think?' or (more exotic) 'are robots conscious?' in terms of how we ought to behave towards them. From the author's point of view, any complex, organised entity deserves some respect, and it would be right to preserve rather than vandalise a complex insect, flower, crystal, or indeed a computer circuit. This is not to say it would not be equally 'logical' to argue that one should do the opposite and go out of one's way to *destroy* such. Against such a view one might perhaps quote Kant, and say that 'one should never act otherwise than so that one could also wish that one's maxim should become a universal law': but a thorough-going vandal might be all for universal vandalism, even though he knew he would find it eventually an uncomfortable world, as Butler's Erewhon was for its native Luddites.

But it seems right to have a 'spectrum' of respect for the rest of creation, with other human beings at the top and grains of sand at the bottom, with computers somewhere in the middle. Certainly the author felt ashamed one night when, working on a computer late at night with little success, he threw a pencil eraser at the central processor in a fit of temper.

Most computer professionals find such discussions rather embarrassing. They are only too aware that their computer system is liable to attacks of abysmal stupidity (as a result of their own errors) and rarely if ever shows signs of independent intelligence. But this does happen, and once or twice a computer solution has emerged which, although the analyst and programmer knew very well how it was arrived at, is nevertheless unexpected and entrancing, like a flight plan which sends the aircraft on an S-curve to avoid headwinds, or a linear program which recommends to a textile company that all sales of garments to big chain stores should be curtailed, or a chess program which sacrifices a queen to mate in three.

Ethics

Computer data-bases can provide authorities with a weapon to use against the individual. Society may be prepared to accept this for the following reasons:

(a) Detection of tax evasion or other crimes/antisocial behaviour
(b) Administrative costs reduced
(c) Provision of help to people who need it (e.g. children needing inoculation)

But as *laymen* we must watch for the following *mis*-uses:

(a) Identification of people who are *not* breaking the law but are disapproved of, e.g. unmarried mothers, tax *avoiders* (as against *evaders*). Recently a government minister stigmatised 'people on the fringe of the law'. This is an alarming attitude. People *outside* the law should be prosecuted, everybody *inside* should be permitted to live their lives: if their neighbours disapprove of them, this should be of no consequence to authority, unless it be to change the law.

(b) Use of information for unsanctioned purposes such as medical information being released to potential employers (even government employers) without the individual's consent, or salaries to credit card companies.

Laymen can take action by quoting instances of malpractice to the press, the Ombudsman, or their MP. The British Computer Society (BCS) also acts as a watchdog on such cases. It has produced a Code of Practice for its members which promotes social responsibility as well as technical competence and good business integrity. Professionals can and should insist on safeguards being built into the systems they introduce, and the BCS will support them if they dig their heels in when they believe they are being asked to do something which is unethical or potentially dangerous to society.

Information is like property and there are very strong feelings involved about letting people, or a computer, have facts about yourself which can be used in ways you cannot control. If we assume that data-bases are necessary for the good of the community, there are two particular safeguards which could be applied:

(a) Everyone should be told exactly what is on file about him or her, and have an independent arbiter to obtain redress if they feel it is incorrect,

(b) The people entitled to get at each piece of information, and the usage, must be defined, and precautions taken to prevent *unauthorised* access or usage, monitored by an independent body. In Scandinavia you have to have an official *licence* to set up a data-base.

These safeguards do, however, mean that the police, social services, the military and industrial companies will have difficulty in keeping information secret when *secrecy* is felt to be in the interests of the community.

Fraud

There are two kinds of fraud involving computers: those in which a computer-based accounting system is penetrated by an embezzler inside (or a crooked supplier/customer outside), and those where a valuable program or piece of equipment is stolen, or the design pirated. The second kind his not particularly interesting, but the first kind does highlight a fault in badly designed computer systems; that is, a failure to define responsibilities. When an accountant introduces a new system, for purchasing, for example, he is responsible for the design, introduction, and security of the system. If it goes wrong, his head rolls. But a computer-based accounting system has the fingers of many specialists in the pie, and often no one man is identifiable as the man to blame if the system fails. An ingenious crook can see where there are gaps in responsibilities: for example, the computer may print out lists of all *new* suppliers for the auditors, but permit *amendments* to be made without such an 'audit trail', so he sets his brother up as a bogus branch of Marks and Spencer, and starts getting money or goods through the system. As with the other objectives of computer-based systems security is achieved by good communication between the people in the project, not by elaborate technical devices. If the computer program refuses access to anyone who does not key in a current password at his terminal, we may not bother to check people playing with the terminal. But they may simply watch what a bona-fide user did to get access, wait for him to go, and press the same keys. As Agesilaus said (according to Plutarch); 'The ramparts of our cities should be built not of stone and timber, but of the brave hearts of our citizens.' All the same, much money is now spent on methods of 'locking out' items of information to unauthorised users: sometimes you are allowed to run a program which can read information, but not change it (e.g. a senior manager checking his employees' salaries), or both read it and change it (e.g. a credit controller examining a customer's credit status). Such devices are *necessary*, like locks on the office confidential filing cabinet, but not altogether *sufficient* to provide security. They have to be part of a security *system*, and a 'system', as we noted at the beginning of this book, is *an organisation of people, each with defined responsibilities, and using appropriate methods, to achieve together a defined set of objectives.*

What the reader should do about computers

In this book the reader has been given only an overall view of computer-based systems, how they are designed and implemented, and what some of the consequences are for the layman. If the reader intends to become a computer professional, and is confident he has the sort of mind which enjoys the cut and thrust of negotiating new systems with management, or the intellectual challenge of communicating with a complicated, literal-minded machine (or both!) then he should start by joining a user or manufacturer company as a trainee analyst or programmer. He should get the job by having qualifications in English, mathematics, a language, and perhaps accountancy, and should be able to talk intelligently about computers. He could not be expected to be able to program already, in fact most employers would be anxious about someone who might have learned bad habits. He will probably be given an aptitude test, and high intelligence is a prerequisite for the job. For a bright school-leaver this is the best and quickest way into computing.

There are a number of firms which teach programming, and certainly a company would look on candidates with approval for having spent their own money on learning. Most such firms provide a free aptitude test before accepting an enrolment, and the reputable ones will advise you if your score indicates you may not succeed. There is a code of practice for computer schools, recommended by the National Computer Centre (NCC), and adopted by the Control Data Institute, London Computer Operators Training Centre, School of Computer Technology, and Computer Programming School. Beware of computer schools who encourage people to pay their fees when their aptitude is not really sufficient, so if you are in doubt, test yourself (e.g. using *Test your own IQ* by Eysenck) as a cross check, and do not embark on a career in computers unless you score well over average.

Alternatively you can enrol at a technical college and learn computing while working in another job, and take examinations leading to a City and Guilds Certificate, 'A' Level, OND Business Studies (Computer Applications), etc. You can also seek full membership of the British Computer Society by external examination.

If your school examination results were good enough, you can enrol as a full-time university student and obtain a degree. At Brunel University, students study full-time and also part of each year working in industry, possibly sponsored by a firm or one of the Armed Services. If you have already spent some years in industry and have a degree or professional institute status, you can study computing on a day-release basis (if your employer will release you one day a week) and obtain a post-graduate degree.

In all cases your local Careers Guidance Centre can put

you in touch with the best institution to help you on your way. Among the Appendices are some examples of examination papers.

After reading this book, you might decide that a career in computing is not for you, because, for example, you already have a satisfying career in another field, but would like to keep abreast of developments because of their intrinsic interest, and because they have so powerful an effect on our society and economic life. You may even feel that it would be fun to do some programming as an amateur. Some reading is suggested in Appendix 7. You may be able to attend computer appreciation courses in your organisation, and your computer manager can probably arrange for you to try your hand at programming, to work out your tax, for example, or simulate a game of cricket.

Layman or professional, you should keep a close eye on what is happening in this field, and do what you can personally to prevent antisocial trends, and encourage those trends in computing which will improve the quality of life: better health, more freedom, more opportunities to stretch ourselves to the full and to work happily with our colleagues—among whom will be, almost certainly, a computer.

Appendix 1

Example of COBOL program sheet

page 150 of IBM F28–8053 COBOL.
(Note that programmers should distinguish 1 and I, 2 and Z, 5 and S, alphabetic O and numeric 0 where ambiguity is possible.)

IBM

COBOL PROGRAM SHEET

```
010   PROCEDURE DIVISION.
020
030   BEGIN.
040     OPEN INPUT PERSONNEL-FILE, OUTPUT RESULT-FILE. MOVE ZERO TO C
050   OUNT.
060   READ-CARDS. READ PERSONNEL-FILE AT END GO TO FINISH.
070     IF (FEMALE
080     AND UNDER-20 IN AGE
090     AND NOT UNDER-5-AND-A-HALF IN HEIGHT
100     AND 185-TO-120 IN WEIGHT
110     AND (CHAZEL OR BROWN IN EYES)
120     AND NOT BALD)
130     OR (MALE
140     AND OVER-50
150     AND OVER-6 (AND OVER-185)
160     THEN ADD 1 TO COUNT. WRITE RESULT-RECORD FROM PERSONNEL-REC
170   ORD.
180     GO TO READ-CARDS.
190   FINISH.
200     DISPLAY 'COUNT IS ', COUNT.
210     CLOSE PERSONNEL-FILE AND RESULT-FILE.
220     STOP RUN.
```

Appendix 2

Example of FORTRAN program sheet

ICL

Fortran
coding
sheet

Title Example
Sheet 1 of 1
Programmer from ICL 4261 (7.71) p 34
Date June 1975

C	STATEMENT NUMBER	CONT.	FORTRAN STATEMENT	IDENTIFICATION AND SEQUENCE No.
C*****		*	SUBROUTINE TO ADD ELEMENTS OF ARRAY I AND RETURN SUM IN J. ***	
C				
			SUBROUTINE ADD(I,J)	
			DIMENSION I(10)	
			J=0	
			DO 2 K=1,10	
			J=J+I(K)	
	2		CONTINUE	
			RETURN	
			END	

FORM 1/5421(9.68)

© International Computers Limited 1964   Printed in Great Britain

Appendix 3

Questions set by Uxbridge Technical College, 1972, internal examination (for A-level students)

SECTION C—DATA PROCESSING

11. Describe a visual display unit and identify the features of a system which makes the use of a visual display unit particularly appropriate. A contracts manager has to be able to offer quick estimates as to the time it will take to produce large quantities of small sub-assemblies. Describe an appropriate computer system which he could use.

12. Distinguish between two methods of on-line data transmission and discuss the communications hardware required by each.

A number of schools are being connected on-line in interactive mode to a large multi-access central processor. State which of the two systems you would select to implement such a scheme, and give reasons for your choice.

13. Describe a technique of preparing data for input to a computer which eliminates the punching of cards, paper tape or documents.

Give one example in which such a technique is used, comment on the integrity of the system and list the advantages and disadvantages associated with it.

14. What are the meanings of the following terms as applied to disc files: (a) selective sequential access, (b) direct access?

Explain methods of file organisation which are designed to take account of the different access requirements. How is overflow in a file area dealt with?

15. In a lamp-making organisation special orders are received for non-standard products. Estimates are required of the time needed to satisfy three of these orders which were received at the same time. Manufacturing resources are limited and production of one item must follow that of another as and when resources become available. The table below sets out the processing time involved in satisfying any one order and the sequence in which these operations are executed.

TABLE 2

Process	Details of process	Time in hours
(a)	To design glassware	8
(b)	To design filament	2
(c)	To produce glassware	24
(d)	To make filaments	56
(e)	To assemble filaments and glassware	4
(f)	To pump lamps and assemble the caps	1
(g)	To test sample of lamps for life and performance	150

Assuming that the processes *within any one order* can only be executed sequentially, but that no other restrictions apply, draw a network representing the production of the three orders and calculate the total time required to complete them. Optimise wherever possible.

Appendix 4

Questions from Part II of British Computer Society
Examination 1973

Option C: Data Processing and Information Systems

PAPER 1

Answer FOUR *questions*

Time: 3 hours

1. You have been retained by a company to advise them
on the possibility of using a computer system to process the
data relating to the firm's activities. The Chairman believes
some other firms of a similar size already have computer
systems in operation, and is concerned in case his firm may
be slipping behind.

What considerations do you think should be taken into
account when deciding whether or not to install a computer?
Relate this question to an area with which you are familiar.

2. What is meant by the term, Data-base Management?
Describe the main features of Data-base Management
systems and indicate the advantages and disadvantages of
such systems from the point of view of
  (i) a user
 (ii) a D.P. Manager
(iii) a Systems Analyst
 (iv) a Programmer
  (v) an Operator

3. Write notes on *three* of the following, illustrating your
answer with examples

(i) key-to-tape (or disc) encoders
(ii) work study
(iii) linear programming
(iv) budgetary control

4. Invasion of privacy by computer-based systems is very topical at the present time.
Discuss the subject indicating two problem areas which can be identified and suggest appropriate solutions.

5. During the initial stages of a project, a detailed investigation of the user area is usually necessary.
Discuss this activity and state your plans for carrying out this systems investigation.

6. The role of the auditor in an organisation has changed with the introduction of computer-based systems.
Discuss and indicate his involvement in the design and implementation of systems.

7. During the system design process it is necessary to specify the criteria for performance of the new system. It may be, for example, that the input error rate could be acceptable at 5% or may have to be taken down to 1%.
Describe, with examples, the other parameters that you would specify.

8. The manufacturers' software is playing a vital role in the present-day computer installation.
Discuss with examples.

PAPER 2

Answer question 1 *and* TWO *other questions*

Time: 3 hours

1. For many years your company has processed all its data by manual methods. A computer has been installed to

assist with an expanding workload and it is intended initially to convert the Payroll, Stock Control and Sales routines from the present manual methods to computer systems.

What problems could arise in the changeover and what checks and procedures would you follow to ensure that the changeover proceeds smoothly?

2. In the feasibility study of a teleprocessing enquiry system it is necessary to quote approximate service times (or turnaround times). Input and output messages are on average 100 characters each, and access to a record on a file is necessary to answer each enquiry.

Calculate a service time, pointing out all the assumptions that you make in your calculations.

3. Describe, with the aid of examples, how you would evaluate the application packages currently available for use on your own company's production control system.

4. 'Indexing is the basic problem, as well as the costliest bottleneck, of information retrieval.'

Elaborate upon the problems of indexing for information retrieval purposes, particularly for mechanical systems.

What recent developments would encourage you to believe that there is a future for automatic retrieval systems?

5. Describe, with examples, the technique known as 'virtual storage'. Identify the advantages and disadvantages as seen by the systems analyst in designing systems.

Appendix 5

Questions from Brunel University final examination for Bachelor of Technology in Computer Science

Brunel University

Bachelor of Technology Degree Examination June 1975
Computer Science (Honours and Ordinary) Part II

COMMERCIAL SYSTEMS   . CS4g

Time allowed 2 hours
Full marks may be obtained for satisfactory answers to about THREE questions

1. An engineering firm maintains a product structure file on disc. Describe how it is likely to be organised, what information it would contain, and how it could be used. Draw a systems flow chart showing its place in the manufacturing control system.

2. Describe three ways in which the financial position of a company might be improved by computer-based sales order processing and invoicing.

3. A computer is used by a large company to pay salaried staff. How could the files and system be extended to help top management plan promotions so as to ensure the right people are in the right jobs? What security problems will arise? How can they be overcome?

4. 'Computers can only predict the future by extrapolating past trends. Today, new factors, known to people but not the computer, are constantly affecting the price and availability of goods. Therefore computer-assisted stock control is worthless.' Discuss.

5. A company believes that it requires a full, 24 hour, reliable real-time system with remote interactive terminals and a centralised data-base on disc, but is alarmed at the costs of the equipment and development. Suggest how costs can be reduced by various compromises, but indicate how these might also reduce benefits.

Appendix 6

Results of stock control bin card exercise

Engines. Minimum Re-order Quantity: 10. Re-order Level: 10

Month	On hand	Issued	Received	Ordered	Costs	Revenue
1	15	12	0	10	18	1800
2	3 + 10	8	10	10	1100 + 18	1200
3	5 + 10	14	10	10	1100 + 16	2100
4	1 + 10	11*	10	10	1100 + 11	1650
5	0 + 10	9	10	10	1100 + 11	1350
6	1 + 10	11*	10	10	1100 + 11	1650
7	0 + 10	10*	10	10	1100 + 10	1500
8	0 + 10	6	10	10	1100 + 14	900
9	4 + 10	13	10	10	1100 + 15	1950
10	1 + 10	11*	10	10	1100 + 11	1650
				TOTALS:	10,035	15,750
						5715 ('profit')

* Unable to satisfy demand

Note that if different Minimum Re-order Quantities and/or Re-order Levels are chosen, the costs and/or revenues can be improved. How about raising them both to 15 for example? This will increase the chance of meeting demand, reduce number of orders placed and thus administrative costs, but *increase* holding costs. (Taking into account the value of extra stock at the end of month 10, the latter policy gives results £1058 better, i.e. an improvement in profitability of 18% on £5715.)

In practice there are statistical methods for arriving at the best values for Re-order Quantity and Re-order Level, but a simulation gives one greater insight into what goes on.

Appendix 7

Recommended reading

Martin, James, *Design of Man–Computer Dialogues* (Prentice-Hall Inc., 1973).

Catt, Ivor, *Computer Worship* (Pitman, 1973).

Wooldridge and London, *The Computer Survival Handbook* (David and Charles, 1973).

Hartman, Matthe, Proeme, *Information Systems Handbook* (Kluwer-Harrap, 1968).

Radford, A. S., *Computer Programming: Fortran* (Teach Yourself Books, 1975).

Appendix 8

Solution to error in Fig. 73

The last malefactor record in the file is never included on any enquiry report. The test for 'last record' should precede instead of follow the READ A MALEFACTOR block.

Index

Note. This index was compiled using some features of a data-base system called CODIL, developed by Dr. C. R. Reynolds, Reader in Computer Science, Brunel University. CODIL has also been used to solve logical puzzles, categorise the fauna in caves, and many other jobs involving logical analysis and searching for information.